THE OUTWARD BOUND

THE OUTWARD BOUND,

CARAVANING
as the Style
of the Church

by
VERNARD ELLER

WILLIAM B. EERDMANS PUBLISHING COMPANY
Grand Rapids, Michigan

Copyright © 1980 by Wm. B. Eerdmans Publishing Co.
255 Jefferson Ave., SE, Grand Rapids, Michigan 49503
Printed in the United States of America

Library of Congress Cataloging in Publication Data

Eller, Vernard.
  The outward bound.

    1.   Church.   2.   Pastoral theology.   I.   Title.
BV600.2.E55   261   79-22927
ISBN 0-8028-1822-6

To my brothers and sisters of
THE FELLOWSHIP
among whom I have caught glimpses
of the vision
presented in this book

Acknowledgments

A number of the ideas in this book (and the actual wording of a few passages) have appeared in earlier works by the author, although they are here given an entirely new and different setting. The "commissary/caravan" model of the church was first used in *Kierkegaard and Radical Discipleship* (Princeton University Press, 1968) and then again in *In Place of Sacraments* (Eerdmans Publishing Company, 1972). The "avant-garde/expediti" model previously appeared as part of an article entitled "The Green Berets of God," in the May 23, 1966, issue of the Church of the Brethren *Messenger.* The "String Quartet/Barbershop-Foursome" model also was used in *In Place of Sacraments.* In the chapter on individual lifestyle, the biblical study of passages from Matthew 6, 12, and 13 is taken from *The Simple Life* (Eerdmans, 1973). Although the dependence is not particularly close, "discipline" and "stripping" were discussed in *The Promise* (Doubleday, 1970). The treatment of Ellul's "Meditation on Inutility" obviously is indebted to that piece from his book *The Politics of God and the Politics of Man* (Eerdmans, 1972). Where appropriate, permission has been obtained from the respective publishers.

Portions of this book also appear in a curriculum resource of the LifeStyle series published by the David C. Cook Publishing Company. Gratitude is expressed to Cook for permitting this simultaneous publication.

Contents

INTROIT:

The Attack and the Attacker

This book can and undoubtedly will be read as an attack upon Christendom. Unfortunately, that title already has been taken. But apart from the incidental consideration that the author of this book is not named Søren Kierkegaard, the difference between the two is that his critique focused upon the claim that there existed a "Christendom," that is, a Christianized *polis* or society expressing itself in the form of an official state church, whereas my critique questions whether what we call "congregations" qualify as being what the New Testament has in mind.

Because this is our topic, and because this book undoubtedly will be read by congregational leaders, both clerical and lay, it seems incumbent upon me to present my qualifications for the task at hand. In my books, articles, and speaking engagements, I am customarily identified as an author, college professor, and at times even "theologian." Yet it is from another, invisible side of my career that I have written the present book.

I am an ordained minister of the Church of the Brethren. I have served (and am serving) in both staff and board positions on the denominational and ecumenical level, and from there have received something of an overview of the congregational life of the churches of Protestantism. I have preached and taught (and still do) in a multitude of congregations which have varied greatly in size and style as well as denominational affiliation. From these experiences, I have at least touched the lives of many members of these groups, and have gained some impressions about what makes these groups tick. I have held membership — and always positions of active participation and leadership — in five different congregations of the Church of the Brethren, ranging from some of the largest and most prestigious to some of the smallest and most humble. I have not only *seen* these congregations, but I have explored them *from the inside.*

But most important, something more than ten years ago, I became one of the founding fathers and volunteer ministers in the Fellowship Church of the Brethren of La Verne, California. The Fellowship, I guess, would have to be called a "rump" congregation, having been conceived and brought into being entirely by its members-to-be, without the sponsorship, strategy planning, or financial assistance of any denominational office. We are a small group (membership of fewer than one hundred and dwindling), but we have worked hard at implementing many of the ideals found in the pages that follow — at becoming a do-it-yourself, de-institutionalized, de-professionalized "people in caravan."

All this is to say that, as an attacker of Christendom, I am at least making the effort to put my money (along with my time, energies, and prayers) where my mouth is. So, know all men by these presents that my intentions are honorable. It is precisely because "beyond my highest joy, I prize her heavenly ways," that I am disturbed when the ways of the church seem so much more worldly than heavenly.

ONE

Three Models for the Church

By "church," let us make clear at the outset that we mean specifically the local congregation, the immediate community of faith. It is at this level that both the author and readers of this book have the most personal responsibility and the greatest chance of having some real effect. If change were to come about at this level, consequent change probably would follow automatically at the level of denominational and ecumenical structures. Likewise, no change at those higher levels would be very significant unless change also took place at the level of the local church.

You probably think we should talk about the lifestyle of the individual Christian before moving on to that of the church. But I am convinced that establishing the proper sort of community is the most critical factor in generating truly Christian lives. Indeed, I would go so far as to say that there is not even the possibility of a fully Christian style of life outside the context of the right sort of Christian community (church).

In this chapter we will examine three basic aspects of the church: (1) its fundamental nature and self-understanding; (2) its relationship to the world, that is, to the society in which it finds itself; and (3) the mode, or style, of its day-to-day operation. We will propose an analogy to help clarify each of these aspects, and in each case the analogy will contrast what the church is and what we propose it should be.

COMMISSARY or CARAVAN?

Where lies the model for a Christian congregation? Where is the church to get a picture of that toward which it should be striving?

From where is it to derive its essential self-understanding?

We propose that the congregations of New Testament times — those that are noted in the New Testament — provide the model. This is not to say that they were model congregations; that obviously was not the case, and Scripture does not present them as being such. But they do represent (however imperfectly) the fresh wineskins fashioned and formed by those who had been directly entrusted by Jesus with the new wine of his gospel. Those churches at least knew what a Christian congregation was supposed to be, whether or not any ever fully succeeded in becoming such a congregation.

Essentially the New Testament pictures the church as a *caravan*. This "caravan" understanding seems to have been normative until the time of Constantine, when Christianity became the official religion of the Roman Empire. This acceptance of Christianity by the world brought with it a different concept of the congregation — a concept which has dominated the church scene to the present day. According to this understanding, the church is pictured basically as a *commissary*.

A *commissary* is an *institution* which has been *commissioned* to *dispense* particular goods, services, or benefits to a *select constituency*. The commissary church, then, sees itself primarily as an institution, a divine institution franchised by God. God has stocked the institution with a supply of heavenly graces (Bible truths, correct theology, the sacraments, etc.) which the clerical proprietors, through proper transaction, can disburse to the customers. The measure of a commissary, it follows, lies in the legality of its franchise, the warranty of its goods, and the authorization of its personnel.

A *caravan,* on the other hand, is something entirely different. It (and a *walking* caravan best fits our idea) is a group of people banded together to make *common cause* in seeking a *common destination*. (Our emphatic use of the word "common" makes it evident that we are speaking of a *community* rather than an *institution*.) The being of a caravan lies not in any signed and sealed authorization but in *the way it functions*. Its validity lies not in its apparatus but in the performance of its caravaners — each and every one of them. A caravan is a caravan only as long as it is making progress — or at least striving to make progress. Once the caravaners stop, dig in, or count themselves as having arrived, they no longer constitute a caravan.

A commissary, for its part, *is* and has its existence simply in being what it is, what God has commissioned it to be. A caravan, conversely, has its existence only in a continual *becoming* (and in allowing that existence continually to be called into question), in a following of the Lord on his way toward the kingdom. With a commissary, the question is: "Has this institution a valid charter, and is it operating within the terms of that charter?" With a caravan, the question is: "How are the people doing? Is the group operating so that all are being helped on their common journey in discipleship?"

A commissary is essentially *establishment* oriented, and a caravan *eschatologically* oriented. The distinction is not simply that of readiness for change. Establishments do change, *have* to change in order to maintain their status as establishments. They change with the times and in the effort to enhance their own size and influence. Yet this is something entirely different from the eschatological concern that could care less about keeping up with the times or enhancing an organization's position. To be following the Lord points the caravan toward a goal that stands beyond history and thus beyond human power to define, project, establish, or effect according to our own desires and devices:

> These all died in faith, not having received what was promised, but having seen it and greeted it from afar, and having acknowledged that they were strangers and exiles on earth. For people who speak thus make it clear that they are seeking a homeland. If they had been thinking of that land from which they had gone out, they would have had opportunity to return. But as it is, they desire a better country, that is, a heavenly one. Therefore God is not ashamed to be called their God, for he has prepared for them a city. —Hebrews 11:13-16

It is perhaps in the concept "membership" that the contrast between commissary and caravan is most stark. In a commissary, a member is essentially a "card carrier," someone who has been certified to enjoy the privileges offered by the institution (without much regard even as to how far the person is actually availing himself of those privileges). In a caravan, on the other hand, "member" has a Pauline, anatomical reference — it means a limb, an appendage, or an organ. A member is seen as an integral, functional, and *functioning* constituent without which the body cannot be the body it was meant to be.

But is the New Testament model all that anti-institutional, all that committed to caravaning? The earliest term used to identify the corporate Christian enterprise (before it was called "a church" or its members called "Christians") was "the Way," its constituents being simply "the followers of the Way," or "those of the Way." The term occurs eight or nine times in the book of Acts (9:2; 18:25, 26; 19:23; 22:4; 24:14, 22) and not elsewhere. However, we should hardly expect to find it elsewhere, Acts being the only account we have of the primitive church. But whether or not these references in Acts can be taken as proof positive that "the Way" was the earliest nomenclature for the church, it is easy to demonstrate that this basic concept underlies much of the New Testament.

A passage from Acts in which the term is not used is the clearest presentation of the idea. It is Stephen's defense before the Sanhedrin in Acts 6:8 — 7:60. The charge brought against Stephen by the Jewish authorities is that he speaks "against this holy place [the temple]" and wants to "alter the customs." It is interesting to note that the controversy does not center on Christian/Jewish differences as such but simply on our two different concepts of the church, or the people of God.

In their protective, custodial concern for holy places and holy customs, the Jews reveal that they have a "commissary" view of the church. They see the church as established, institutionalized, settled, and fixed.

Stephen, in his turn, is determined to show that the church is called to be a "caravan"; the first characteristic of the people of God is that they ever are "on the way" and never secure in a state of accomplishment. He begins by using Abraham as a model and makes it clear that his significance is as one who continually has to get up and go in response to the forward call of God. He passed through much territory but had "nothing in it to call his own, not one yard." All he had was a "promise" of possession addressed to him and his posterity.

Stephen then moves to the story of Joseph where the theme again is that God's people have no abiding place but must live the lives of wanderers. This brings him to the archetypal "going out," or the exodus from Egypt. At this point Stephen introduces a second theme, a negative one, namely the people's desire to stay put, their resistance against any call that meant pulling up stakes and hitting the road. The key verse here is 7:25. Describing Moses' killing of the Egyptian taskmaster, Stephen says, "He thought his fellow-countrymen would understand that God was offering them deliverance through him, but they did not understand." This dialectic between God's offer to lead the way to deliverance and the people's failure to follow that lead governs the remainder of the passage.

In this regard, it should be made very clear that we are not at all suggesting that the modern church should switch to a caravan model for the purpose of making the church more successful and attractive for Christians or people in general. On the contrary, to be part of a caravan is much more demanding than joining the clientele of a commissary. Given a choice, "the people" will go for the commissary every time. That is why Moses got the reaction he did. This is why Stephen's opponents reacted the way they did. That is why the church is where it has been since the time of Constantine. The church is smart enough to see what works best with the people. If there is to be a new move toward caravaning in our day, it can and should come only out of a sense that this is what Jesus asks of us.

"This Moses," Stephen says in verse 35, "whom they rejected . . . was commissioned as ruler and liberator [leader-lord] by God himself." Then, in verse 37, comes the heart of the entire argument: "It was he again who said to the Israelites, 'God will raise up a prophet for you from among yourselves as he raised me.'" Stephen's intent is clear: Moses' significance is as a leader-lord, not as the guarantor of holy places and holy customs. Further, as per the quotation from Deuteronomy, Moses foretold that in due time God would raise up a new, eschatological leader-lord. Obviously, Stephen is identifying Jesus as this new leader-lord. But just as the Israelites did not understand that through the first Moses God was leading them in the way of deliverance, so now their descendants will not recognize the new Moses.

Beginning in verse 44, Stephen again uses the dialectic. Under Moses, "our forefathers had the Tent of the Testimony in the desert." This tent is the proper form of a church for a people on the way; the church is as mobile, as adaptable, as ready for change as the people themselves. But Israel could not be content with this, so Solomon had to go and build a house for God — even though Scripture says that "the Most High does not live in houses made with hands." "How stubborn you are, heathen still at heart and deaf to the truth! You always fight against the Holy Spirit. Like fathers, like sons." When God sends a leader-lord who says, "OK, let's go!" you say, "Let's stay! The Lord is in his holy temple — and besides, we like it here!"

Stephen's defense was very effective: it got him stoned to death, which is a good indication that he had won the debate and that his opponents could not find any other way to answer him. It is also apparent that he was interpreting the Bible just exactly right.

Throughout the Old Testament (and rather prominently in the New) we see that the archetype of salvation is the Passover and the exodus event. If that be so, then it is plain that salvation cannot be understood as a state of having it made, of settling down to enjoy a condition of secure accomplishment. Instead, salvation is the experience of being made free to travel, of being called out by a leader-lord and enabled to follow him on his way to the kingdom. The people of God who are the church should, in their institutions and life together, show forth something of this understanding.

With that, we have made our best effort in establishing the distinction between a commissary and a caravan church. It is up to you to decide how this applies to your particular congregation and what, if anything, is to be done about it. Undoubtedly different congregations represent different shades or mixtures of the two types.

But as you do your analysis, be aware that the basic distinction has its effect on almost every aspect of congregational life and structure; even small details can be revealing of the premises that lie behind a congregation's self-understanding. Be alert to these. Be ready to follow out all the ramifications. For instance, the pastor is probably going to project a very different image if he sees himself as the appointed proprietor of a divine establishment than if he sees himself as a leader who is essentially one of the caravaners making his own journey along with his brothers and sisters.

What about buildings? Does caravaning suggest that the congregation will have to renounce buildings and begin meeting in tents? Probably not. But there is no escaping the fact that the two views of the church will lead the congregation to a different understanding of how much the church ought to be identified with its buildings. If a visitor saw only your church buildings, what would he deduce about the character of your church? Commissary or caravan, there is bound to be a difference in priorities, in the amount of money, attention, and pride invested in buildings.

Perhaps it should be pointed out that the distinction we are making between commissary and caravan churches will not begin to match up with the distinction between theologically liberal and conservative churches; this distinction cuts right across that one. We are not taking *theological* sides at any point in this study.

AVANT-GARDE or EXPEDITI?

Both of the terms above identify military units — which makes them apt for comparison and contrast. It will soon become obvious that this pair correlates very well with our commissary/caravan pair; yet they address themselves to different issues. In this section we will be talking about two different ways in which the church sees itself related to the society in which it finds itself.

Avant-garde combines the French words meaning *before* and *guard*. Originally it referred to the foremost part of an army, those troops that lead the way, take the first shocks of encounter with the enemy, set the pattern of battle, and establish the situation for the main force that comes behind. However, more recently the word has been used in relation to art, literature, and music. It has come to mean cultural leadership. Theologian Harvey Cox spoke explicitly of "the church as God's avant-garde" in his best-seller of a decade or so ago entitled *The Secular City*.

On the other hand, Søren Kierkegaard, the Danish thinker of more than a century ago, spoke of the church as being made up of *expediti*. *Expediti* combines the Latin *ex* ("out of," as in "exclude," to include someone *out*) and *ped* ("foot," as in "*pedal*," to foot it around and around). Accordingly, it means "out of foot," or more accurately, "freed feet," or "those who are free of foot." An "expedition," it follows, is a trip taken by those who are free of foot. The term originated with the military machine that created and ruled the Roman Empire. It was used in reference to certain crack army corps, at the special disposition of the emperor, so organized and outfitted to get on their feet and into action effectively and *fast*. The American Expeditionary Forces of World War I probably would not qualify — although they were named right. Closer to the idea are some of the Special Forces and Task Forces of contemporary military and police organizations.

Consider, then, that the nature and position of the *avant-garde* must be defined in relation to the army proper; "the guard before" has to imply the presence of "a mass behind." The very term "avant-garde" carries with it a certain pride of position, the vanity of believing that we are today where the common run of people may get tomorrow — with our help and guidance. When avant-garde is understood in its *artistic* context, this pride of place becomes particularly acute. Overtones of sophistication, superior intelligence, and foresight inevitably lead to a scornfulness toward all the old fuddy-duddies who have not made it to the front line.

Yet the truth of the matter is that the avant-garde is totally tied to and dependent upon those fuddy-duddies. It can be defined only in relation to them. Thus, in order even to *be* avant-garde, attention must be paid to which way the world is going, so that one can stay *in front*. The avant-garde continually must look back to see whether the world is following. The avant-garde must continually seek out the new because if the masses ever caught up with it, there would no longer be an avant-garde. And the avant-garde must continually take care that it is leading where the masses *will* follow, that it is selling what the masses *will* buy; otherwise it loses its reason for being, its function as social leader.

The concept *"expediti,"* however, includes no orientation of this sort. Nothing is even implied about the presence of other troops. *Expediti* operate as a self-defined unit, independent of where the masses may be, or what the masses may be doing. But a self-defined avant-garde would be a contradiction in terms.

If *"expediti"* implies any orientation at all, it is toward the Emperor. The *expediti* are ready, unencumbered, unentangled, uncommitted (in one sense), precisely so that they can give the Emperor (who represents their one, total commitment) instant obedience. When the command comes to move, they move. There is no looking back to see whether anyone is following their lead, no need to compare their position with that of anyone else, for they are under orders. There is no temptation to take pride in their position. The most *expediti* can hope to achieve is the fulfilling of their orders. There is no common standard by which to measure their achievement over against the achievements of others (who knows what the Emperor wants from them?). Both the motivation and the goal of the *expediti* are entirely different from that of the avant-garde.

As we come now to compare the New Testament church with these models, the first thing to be said is that there is a sense in which that church *could* accurately have been called "the avant-garde," and would have welcomed such a label. These early Christians firmly believed that "the way" God was taking them was "the way" he intended eventually and ultimately for all mankind. Revelation 14:4 says that Christians "have been ransomed as the firstfruits of humanity for God and the Lamb."

However, they saw this as happening through the action of God and because it was his will — and not at all as a result of their own brilliant leadership. Above all, they had no inclination to adapt their way to what the world would most likely follow. They were not, then, an avant-garde in the sense we have been using the term. They came closer to being the kind of church that Paul describes: "as the scum of the world, the dregs of all things, even until now" (1 Cor. 4:13). This church obviously was not making any effort to be recognized as a social leader.

The crux of the matter is that to go avant-garde would have been an exact reversal of the relationship Jesus had prescribed in John 17:16-18. There the disciples had been told that they were to be "*in* the world but not *of* the world." The *expediti* role would seem to qualify here. Jesus' words were: "As thou didst send me into the world, I also have sent them into the world." This is precisely the way in which *expediti* are *in* the world, sent at the command of the Emperor to do his bidding and accomplish his work. Likewise, *expediti* are not *of* the world, that is, their goals and values center entirely in the will of the Emperor and bear no relationship to what the world may call good or be on the way to calling good.

The avant-garde, on the other hand, sees things the opposite way. If, by definition, it is *ahead* of the world, it cannot at the same time be *in* the world. Indeed, its pride of place comes precisely from the certainty that where it is at is *not* where the world is at.

Conversely, the avant-garde is very much *of* the world in the sense that its goals and values are determined totally by its relationship to the world — by trying to place itself where the world will want to be. There should be little question as to which of the roles complies with the call of Jesus and the model of the New Testament church.

In a succeeding chapter, we will examine these things from a different angle, and will pick up this line of thought and carry it much further. At this point you are asked only to make an assessment of your own congregation, and to judge how many and what decisions regarding your church's life and conduct are made solely out of a desire to be obedient to the Lord, and how many are made with an eye to "looking good" by the norms and standards of society.

We need to be especially warned not to fall into the liberal/conservative trap in this regard. Conservative churches tend to be very sensitive to the worldlinesses of the liberals, liberals tend to be very sensitive to the worldlinesses of the conservatives, and each tends to be blind to its own worldliness. But as with commissary/caravan, we contend that the avant-garde/*expediti* distinction will not begin to correspond to the traditional theological categories.

Of course, the term "avant-garde" has tended to be the very label and pride of the *liberal* left wing, and this somewhat complicates our analysis. But we need to understand that our *definition* of avant-garde can be applied across the board.

The liberal church, I would suggest, tends to be worldly by allowing the church to become identified with the world's left-wing social causes — and more particularly, the world's left-wing socio-political *techniques*. Likewise, it tends to identify with the world's liberal, permissive moral standards.

However, although it may require a real mental adjustment to see it so, it is also evident that the conservative church is just as avant-garde in identifying itself with *right-*wing political causes and techniques. Just like the liberals, the conservatives see their church in the forefront of society, leading it in the direction it is moving. And much more conspicuously, the conservative (evangelical) church is borrowing from the world and even leading the world by staging mass rallies, producing television spectaculars, using the super-popular musical idiom of the moment in the service of the gospel, and enlisting the avant-garde talents and reputations of political luminaries, movie stars, beauty queens, and sports heroes. All of this projects an avant-garde image of the church.

Making the avant-garde/*expediti* assessment of the church will call for some brutal honesty as well as broad vision and profound insight.

THE ROYAL VIENNA STRING QUARTET
or
A BARBERSHOP FOURSOME?

This pair will correlate nicely with both the avant-garde/*expediti* and the commissary/caravan analogies. In fact, what we actually may be doing is simply following out implications of the basic commissary/caravan dichotomy. In any case, now we shall examine the style of operation that characterizes the internal functioning of the congregation.

Although both the Vienna and the barbershop groups are quartets dedicated to the making of music, that is about the extent of their commonality. In truth, they exist for different ends and must be evaluated by different criteria. The purpose of the Vienna Quartet is to produce music of *the highest possible quality* for the enjoyment of *the audience*. On the contrary, the purpose of the barbershop group is to have *a satisfying experience of singing* (or, to put it honestly, "just plain fun"), not for the sake of any audience but *for their own benefit*. The *quality* of the music is of comparatively little concern. The contrast is between "do it yourself," participatory, amateur performance in the one case and "nothing but the best," spectator-oriented, professional performance in the other. Obviously, each style has its place; the question is, "Which is most appropriate to the fresh wineskins of the church of Jesus Christ?"

In order to insure the quality of its performance, what must the Vienna Quartet do? It places as many aspects of the production as possible into the hands of professionally trained personnel — this includes not only the musicians but also the advance man, publicist, booking agent, house manager, light man, stage crew, ushers, ticket sellers, and others. All the appurtenances of the physical setting must be "right." Professional expertise is sought at every level of the operation.

Now, regarding the church, it is in a congregation's practice of public worship that the Vienna/barbershop distinction will become most visible. And within worship, the manner of observing the Lord's Supper is probably the dead giveaway. (I have written an entire book, *In Place of Sacraments*, chasing the commissary/caravan distinction through baptism and the Lord's Supper). But although the contrast is most conspicuous in worship, our distinction will more than likely be apparent in all the programs of the church — Christian education, business meetings, and so forth. From top to bottom, a congregation will tend to be either an organization run professionally for the sake of the spectators or a group of people doing their own thing for the fun of it.

Yet look at the most common of our worship traditions and be struck with the Vienna Quartet parallels! Our sanctuaries are designed as religious concert halls. In many cases they are even more resplendent (and expensive) than their secular counterparts. The clergy try to perform as smoothly and impressively as professional musicians. The cadence of the liturgy and the grace of the ritual are designed to create an effect not essentially different from that for which the Vienna Quartet (or perhaps the Moscow Ballet) strives. The distinction we are pressing is not necessarily the distinction between formal and more informal worship. Just because the pastor affects a Lawrence Welk or Johnny Carson mode rather than that of a Vienna Quartet member does not mean that he is on the barbershop side of the line. He is obviously playing to a different audience, but the one represents as much of studied, professional showmanship as the other.

Consider specifically, then, the Lord's Supper. There is not the slightest doubt that the early Christians celebrated it while sitting (or reclining) around tables. The eucharist itself was part of a real supper, a full meal, the love feast or *agapé*. These were caravaners gathered as the community of the Lord, celebrating that community, and *demonstrating* community. The service took place while looking in the eye a brother or sister you knew by name (and more than just by name), breaking bread with him or her, and even exchanging the holy kiss.

Yet look at what the Vienna Quartet commissary has done to this most central symbol of the church! It can hardly be said anymore that the *congregation* celebrates the Lord's Supper. The cleric does the celebrating while the congregation looks on as an admiring audience. The people do *take* communion, of course, but not any differently from the way they took in the music in the concert hall the night before. The term *eucharist* means "to show good favor, gratitude, or thanksgiving." As such, it points toward *the people* expressing *their* thanks through *their* actions and words — not through a professional delivering beautiful declamations from a manual.

Plainly, a primary requisite for "barbershopping" will be to get the pastor down off the stage and out of the spotlight. It might be more appropriate to suggest that the congregation get up on the stage with the pastor — except that the whole concert hall image is wrong in any case. Søren Kierkegaard was perhaps the first to see this:

> Alas, in regard to things spiritual, the foolishness of many is this, that they in the secular sense look upon the speaker as an actor, and the listeners as theatergoers who are to pass judgment upon the artist. But the speaker is not the actor — not in the remotest sense. No, the speaker is the prompter. There are no theatergoers present, for each listener will be looking into his own heart. The stage is eternity, and the listener, if he is the true listener (and if he is not, he is at fault) stands before God during the talk. . . . The address is not given for the speaker's sake, in order that men may praise or blame him. The listener's repetition of it is what is aimed at. . . . In the theater, the play is staged before an audience who are called theatergoers; but at the devotional address, God himself is present. In the most earnest sense, God is the critical theatergoer, who looks on to see how the lines are spoken and how they are listened to. . . . The listener, if I may say so, is the actor, who in all truth acts before God.[1]

Now of course, the pastor is one member of the barbershop quartet. Quite properly the pastor may be the one who gives the pitch and downbeat, but the pastor is not to be the whole show. There is no reason why he or she should be dressed differently (vestments) or act as though his or her function were essentially different from anyone else's function. In fact, the pastor should

[1]*Purity of Heart Is to Will One Thing,* pp. 180-81.

deliberately work at subduing the "performer" image and play up the actions of the group itself. From its beginnings, Protestantism has had a very nice doctrine of the priesthood of all believers. The only trouble is that the actual style of our congregational life most often gives the lie to the doctrine we profess.

The Vienna/barbershop contrast has some clear implications regarding the physical arrangement of our churches. I am not necessarily implying that it would be easy or even practical to make things a great deal different than they are, but we should at least be aware that the symbolism is all wrong. For one thing, the sanctuary rather than the fellowship hall is seen as the center of the church. For another thing, most of those sanctuaries are quite lavish and luxurious, and not exactly reminiscent of a suffering-servant Lord in caravan with his people. And finally, they are arranged incorrectly. Concert halls simply are not designed for communal activity; they are designed to expedite what is essentially private experience. The only people facing one another are the performer up front and each individual member of the audience on his or her own line of sight. At a concert, it makes not the slightest difference whether you have any personal relationship with the other people present. And the tragedy, of course, is not so much that the sanctuaries are wrong as that what we do in them is so appropriate to that setting.

A Vienna Quartet performance is not a celebration of community; a barbershop get-together, on the other hand, is — an activity of a people in community with their Lord and with one another in him. There is no doubt at all as to where the New Testament church stood on this one. Here were congregations that owned no property at all, let alone the finest buildings in town. They met in homes (or catacombs) and were prepared to start enough such house churches to care for the Christian constituency of a locale. It was only when the church switched from caravan to commissary that it also began to form large congregations. A question to consider is: "How large can a congregation get without losing its 'barbershop' possibilities and inevitably slipping into a Vienna Quartet mode?" (It is evident, of course, that a congregation can be a Vienna Quartet as soon as it has as many as four members; smallness of size does not automatically make "barbershopping" the order of the day.)

The early Christian barbershoppers had no professional staffs (or octaves) to make their music for them. They were "do it yourself" organizations, sometimes *in extremis*. Paul, apparently, would convert a few people, start a congregation, and then move on. At times he would leave or send one of his helpers to give some leadership, and sometimes the new Christians were entirely on their own. In any case, it is plain that the people did their own "doing" rather than hiring experts to do it for them.

The one specific description of worship in the early church is from 1 Corinthians 14:26-33:

> *What then, brethren? When you come together, each one has a hymn, a lesson, a revelation, a tongue, or an interpretation. Let all things be done for edification. If any speak in a tongue, let there be only two or at most three, and each in turn; and let one interpret. But if there is no one to interpret, let each of them keep silence in church and speak to himself and to God. Let two or three prophets speak, and let the others weigh what is said. If a revelation is made to another sitting by, let the first be silent. For you can all prophesy one by one, so that all may learn and all be encouraged; and the spirits of prophets are subject to prophets. For God is not a God of confusion but of peace.*

As the Corinthians apparently had amply demonstrated, the danger in allowing people to do their own worshiping was that of confusion and disorder. But would Paul have approved of taking worship out of the hands of the people and giving it to professionals?

Acts 2:42-47 describes the broader life of an early congregation:

> *They met constantly to hear the apostles teach, and to share the common life, to break bread, and to pray. A sense of awe was everywhere, and many marvels and signs were brought about through the apostles. All whose faith had drawn them together held everything in common: they would sell their property and possessions and make a general distribution as the need of each required. With one mind they kept up their daily attendance at the temple, and, breaking bread in private houses, shared their meals with unaffected joy, as they praised God and enjoyed the favor of the*

whole people. And day by day the Lord added to their number those whom he was saving.

Now it can be (and has been) endlessly debated whether community of goods is a proper practice and one incumbent upon modern Christians. This makes a good debate — because few if any of the debaters would be willing to give serious consideration to practicing community of goods anyway. So let us move away from matters of theory and center our debate on the issue that is much more relevant to what we might actually do and much more germane to the biblical text: Does the Acts passage suggest that the early church was more strongly oriented toward a Vienna Quartet model or a barbershop foursome model? Or to put it more bluntly: is there in either passage the hint of anything except full-fledged barbershopping?

As we come, then, to measure our own contemporary congregations against the New Testament's "fresh wineskins," there is one convenient way of evading the resultant (and very painful) contrast. It can be argued that the New Testament model is simply impractical, unrealistic, and inappropriate for our day and situation. Still, this cannot justify what the church has chosen to become. There is plenty of room to be different from the New Testament model without deserting "barbershopping" or becoming a Vienna Quartet.

Even if the congregation may own property and facilities, what does that have to do with luxurious concert halls and the performances that take place in them? Even if the church may have a trained and salaried ministry, what has that to do with our setting up professionals as performers whose religious spectacles we can watch without having to do any performing ourselves? Even if the ownership of goods may be by individual Christians rather than by the church body, what has that to do with the congregation's eagerness to be recognized as a Royal Vienna String Quartet?

Take a good, honest look at the style of your own congregational life. Decide whether you need or want to make a move toward "barbershopping." Consider how your church might make such a move.

TWO

Faith or Calculation?

In the next chapter, we are going to identify the church's having switched its basic interest from "fidelity" to "success" as the root of its identity crisis. However, we will be in better position to understand that matter if we can see that lying behind it is an even more fundamental confusion, one between "faith" and "calculation." What most people understand as "faith" perhaps should more accurately be called "calculation."

At least for me, the insight has been most clearly revealed in a poem by Robert Browning, entitled "Bishop Blougram's Apology." The poem itself is much too long and, as with a great deal of Browning's work, much too obtuse to be of direct help. Consequently, I will condense, paraphrase, and interpret Browning to fit our purposes. The title of the poem, by the way, uses "apology" in the sense of "defense, explanation, or rationale" rather than "saying you're sorry." The bishop will be obeying the biblical injunction to give a reason for the hope (faith) that is in him — though this is not to say that his faith is a proper one.

This work is an example of what Browning did best; his "dramatic monologues" are poems spoken entirely by one character. The speaker is in conversation, intending to communicate one thing but accidentally revealing his true character in the process. Thus the listener *hears* something entirely different from what the speaker *thought* he was saying. Undoubtedly the same thing often happens in real life.

The setting of the poem is the nineteenth century (Browning's own day). A Roman Catholic bishop, Sylvester Blougram, invites a young, aspiring journalist, Mr. Gigadibs, into his quarters. Blougram discerns (probably correctly) that Gigadibs is a non-Christian humanist who is totally dedicated to the ideals of truth, honesty, and justice, and whose great dream is to become a world-renowned author who promotes these ideals. Blougram also knows that Gigadibs thinks that he, the bishop, is a shyster. And Blougram's idea is to toy with Gigadibs a bit, match wits with him, establish the superiority of the bishop's own philosophy of life, puncture the young man's idealistic naivete, and put him in his place.

Throughout the poem, the bishop sees himself as both a representative and an exemplar of the Christian faith. What we (and Gigadibs) discover is that, in reality, the bishop represents only self-serving calculation. And the difference between these two qualities is absolute. Browning leaves it to his readers to define "faith." But to do it for him, faith can be defined as concentrated, unqualified *choice*, total *commitment*, radical *venture* in the face of all risk, going all out and burning your bridges behind you. Blougram's "calculation," on the other hand, shows up precisely as figuring percentages, playing it smart, minimizing risks, keeping options open, and always looking for the advantage.

Early on, Blougram introduces his own basic premise in a parable that will prove to be the key to the poem as a whole:

> A simile!
> We mortals cross the ocean of this world
> Each in his average cabin of a life;
> The best's not big, the worst yields elbow-room.
> Now for our six months' voyage — how prepare?
>   (ll. 99-103)

Gigadibs with his idealistic dreams, the bishop suggests, would try to bring with him on the voyage Persian rugs, a piano, a whole library of books, a marble bathtub — everything a person could desire. And the captain, then, would meet him saying, "Six feet square! If you won't understand what six feet means, and compute and purchase stores accordingly, well, then, you won't be allowed to bring on anything!"

The bishop, on the other hand, being above all a practical man, is willing to settle for much less, though actually coming off with much more. He has figured out the optimum way of outfitting a cabin — going for what is possible, achieving it, and then enjoying it. There is certainly nothing to criticize in that, is there?

But where do faith and Christianity come in?

Just here. Blougram first argues that by nature there is no such thing as a total and true "believer" (as he himself appears to be); we all have some points of doctrine upon which we are nagged by lingering doubts. But neither, he adds, is there by nature any such thing as a total "unbeliever" (as Gigadibs claims to be). Gigadibs must be bothered by possibilities that Christianity *might* be true as much as Blougram is bothered by possibilities that it might *not* be true. This means, then, that the evidence does not automatically compel anyone to be either a believer or non-believer. In his own mind and experience, each person has grounds for going one way as well as the other. How one makes the choice is determined by something other than the evidence itself.

Well obviously, Blougram concludes, in such a case what else is there to do but to use the old noggin, figure the odds, and go with the choice that best promises to pay off? Which is the better furniture piece for a ship's cabin — belief or unbelief? And on that basis, Blougram maintains, the only possible choice is clearly Christian belief.

And if it is smart to assent to Christian belief, the bishop proceeds, then it is doubly smart to adhere totally to that Christian belief — decisiveness beats indecision every time. Indeed, one advantage of his own Roman Catholicism, the bishop says, is that the church has defined down to the finest detail everything a Christian should or should not believe. And so, in Blougram's case, if the church says there is a cathedral somewhere with a statue of the Virgin that cries real tears on occasion, the bishop believes that this is so — without question.

Oh, sure, he is quick to admit that he has doubts at times. But he is smart enough to keep things to himself and confine them to dreams at night — a much better move than Gigadibs' taking his doubts into the daylight and making them the basis of his public stance.

And look at the results! Because he is a true believer of the Christian faith, Blougram has become a bishop. He always has had a love of power, a need to dominate and control others. Now he can do it without having to be an inelegant, brutal tyrant. Instead, people now come to him — a man of God — on their knees, pleading for him to tell them what to do and where to go. Also, he can enjoy nice clothes without any fear of being accused of vanity. In fact, the people will give him robes and jewels to accent his spiritual standing and responsibility.

So, Bishop Blougram has both the unthinking masses and his own ecclesiastical colleagues starry-eyed in their adoration of his Christian faith and his finesse in using it. But, Gigadibs would probably ask, what about the truly smart people, the intellectuals who *know* that this Christianity stuff is all a bunch of jazz? Where does Blougram stand with them?

Blougram claims that he has solved this problem, too. He plays his role so well that intellectuals simply will not be able to decide whether he stands with the idiot masses, believing all that they do, or whether he actually is one with the intellectuals themselves, intelligent enough not to believe but also smart enough to act as though he did. Why, even the bishop's enemies must admire him for being so shrewd in working things so as to come out on top, whether or not the faith is true. Indeed, Blougram thinks that Gigadibs himself will finally be forced to take this view of the matter.

The bishop then cites a couple of historical examples to show how completely he has covered his bases. Blougram's model is Martin Luther. Luther chose to be a man of great Christian faith, started a whole new church movement, and won not only the love and following of the masses, but also a secure place of honor in world history. The sad thing is that Luther did the new Christian movement bit without allowing Blougram a shot at it.

Yet over against Luther put a nineteenth-century scholar named David Friedrich Strauss, a skeptic who set out to prove that the Gospels' portrayal of Jesus was a false one. This, in Blougram's opinion, was a completely stupid move; there is no percentage in *attacking* the faith. Even for those who agreed with Strauss, there was no particular reason for them to admire, follow, or honor him. He could never hope for the sort of lasting reputation that Luther had.

Old Blougram thought of everything; consider this one. Suppose — it's an outside chance — but just suppose Christianity is right about there being a life after death. Luther lost no advantage in this life by believing that there was. And if, at death, it turned out that he was wrong and there was no afterlife, he was no worse off than he would have been anyway. But if it turned out that he was right and there is an afterlife, one certainly could do worse than to go in as Martin Luther, the great believer. (And it wouldn't hurt to go in as a Roman Catholic bishop, either.)

But then consider poor David Friedrich Strauss. Even if he was right that there is no life after death, believing so gained him no advantage for this life. Neither did he gain any advantage in death. And if Strauss was wrong and there *is* an afterlife, going in as a skeptic and unbeliever is hardly a propitious move. No, Luther definitely has the better of Strauss. Refusal to believe cannot carry any advantage however one looks at it. Willingness to believe carries all the advantage, no matter what the truth proves to be.

> Of course you are remarking all this time
> How narrowly and grossly I view life,
> Respect the creature-comforts, care to rule
> The masses, and regard complacently
> "The cabin," in our old phrase. Well I do.
> I act for, talk for, live for this world now,
> As this world prizes action, life and talk:
> No prejudice to what next world may prove,
> Whose new laws and requirements, my best pledge
> To observe then, is that I observe these now,
> Shall do hereafter what I do meanwhile.
> Let us concede (gratuitously though)
> Next life relieves the soul of body, yields
> Pure spiritual enjoyment: well, my friend,
> Why lose this life i' the meantime, since its use
> May be to make the next life more intense?
> (ll. 764-79)

Finally, the bishop winds up his argument with a decisive demonstration of how absolutely superior his achievement *through faith* is to what Gigadibs represents. He dares (indeed, he invites) Gigadibs to write up and publish whatever he pleases concerning what Blougram has said. Nobody would believe it. Blougram's own people, of course, would take Gigadibs for a liar, knowing that their beloved bishop would never say anything of the sort. But even the bishop's enemies would not believe Gigadibs because they know that Blougram certainly is not foolish enough to say such things to a newspaper reporter.

> Go write your lively sketches! be the first
> "Blougram, or The Eccentric Confidence"—
> Or better simply say, "The Outward Bound"
> [in reference, of course, to the metaphorical cruise
> in the ship's cabin].   (ll. 961-63)

Though we must be struck by the wrongness of it all, Blougram has posed an argument that is very difficult to rebut. Our first inclination, I am sure, is to say, "But Blougram doesn't *really* believe!" Yet Blougram insists that he does, that he has deliberately chosen to believe (and don't we all believe by *choosing* to?). What evidence is there that he is not telling the truth? The poem carries no hint that there is anything in the bishop's life that is inconsistent with his profession of faith.

And yet Browning (as was his custom) closes the poem with a brief, nine-line hooker that effectively cuts Blougram off at the knees and exposes his error:

> He [Gigadibs] did not sit five minutes. Just a week
> Sufficed his sudden healthy vehemence.
> Something had struck him in the "Outward-bound"
> Another way than Blougram's purpose was:
> And having bought, not cabin-furniture
> But settler's-implements (enough for three)
> And started for Australia — there, I hope,
> By this time he has tested his first plough,
> And studied his last chapter of St. John.
>   (ll. 1006-14)

Gigadibs had suddenly seen the *truth* and thus the fatal flaw upon which the bishop had based his entire philosophy. It has to do with the parable of the ocean voyage.

From the outset Blougram assumed that the voyage of this life is a *cruise,* that is, a going whose only purpose is to enjoy the activity of *going,* not necessarily arriving anywhere in particular. And on that assumption, the bishop is right; on a cruise, play things so as to get maximum satisfaction from the cruise itself. But what if it should be, as Gigadibs sees in his sudden healthy vehemence, that life is migration toward *a port*? Then priorities are immediately reversed. Whether or not the cabin is comfortable is now only a minor consideration. All that counts is that one be carrying whatever is necessary for life in the new homeland — "settler's-implements," if you will.

Even though Browning names Australia as Gigadibs' destination, it is not necessary to think of this as a voyage through *space*, which is headed toward a pearly-gated city somewhere. I am virtually certain that the New Jerusalem is *not* in Australia. But if we understand this voyage as a voyage through *time* — taking our cue from Jesus' suggestion that "Thy kingdom come" *is* "Thy will being done *on earth*" — then it seems plain that Australia *will* have its place in the kingdom of God. Yet, with Australia in or out, the kingdom of God (his will being done on earth) is the destination of this world's life and existence. The New Testament makes that clear whether Browning does or not.

That Gigadibs takes implements "enough for three" may mean that he plans to start a family or it may mean only that he will be there for some time. In either case, we have a symbol of permanence, of a true destination, over against the obvious transiency of Blougram's *cruise*, during which one uses each moment for what one can get out of it. Gigadibsians are caravaners and not cruisers; "they are seeking a homeland, the city which has foundations, whose builder and maker is God" (Heb. 11:8-16).

I see the reference to Gigadibs' testing of his first plough as a reminder of Jesus' words, "No one who sets his hand to the plough and then keeps looking back is fit for the kingdom of God" (Lk. 9:62). How could Browning's point be stated any better? The Christian life is to be lived exclusively with a vision of the end, with eyes fixed solely on the kingdom, and precisely not, like Blougram, looking back and around to catch all the angles and to figure all the odds.

Gigadibs' study of the last chapter of St. John would seem to point us to John 21:18-23. There Jesus says to Peter:

> "And further, I tell you this in very truth: when you were young you fastened your belt about you and walked where you chose; but when you are old you will stretch out your arms, and a stranger

*will bind you fast, and carry you where you have no wish to go."
He said this to indicate the manner of death by which Peter was to
glorify God. Then he added, "Follow me."*

*Peter looked round, and saw the disciple whom Jesus loved
following – the one who at supper had leaned back close to him to
ask the question, "Lord, who is it that will betray you?" When he
caught sight of him, Peter asked, "Lord, what will happen to
him?" Jesus said, "If it should be my will that he wait until I come,
what is it to you? Follow me."*

Blougram is the youngster who is his own man, picking his
own shots, going his own way. But Gigadibs is committed; he has
made the venture that leaves him no option but to follow Jesus,
whether the course meets his preferences or not, whether it be
pleasant or hard. And for such *expediti,* there is no looking back
either to worry about or wait for Blougrams, beloved disciples, or
anyone else. To take the Precursor of the Kingdom at his word and
to *follow him* is enough for a Gigadibs.

Unbeknownst to Browning, a contemporary German pastor, Christoph Blumhardt, stated in a word the different orientation of a Blougram and a Gigadibs.

> "Lo, I am with you always, even unto the end of the world"
> (Matthew 28:20). The Savior's being with us has reference
> to the end of the world [i.e., its goal or destiny], not its
> continuance. . . . Jesus is not *with* a person who spends his
> days for the sole purpose of sustaining his earthly life. The
> Lord does not wish to spend too much effort on the ongoing
> of the world. After all, it is all corruptible, and there is
> nothing left to be done but to wait the wearing out of the
> decaying structure and the creating of a new one. For the
> time being we must do the best we can with what we have.
> . . . [But] in all our work let us be careful to fix our eyes not
> on the continuance of the world, but on its end.

And unbeknownst to you, after our run through this chapter
we have arrived back at home plate, as it were. For what sort of
church continually refers to the kingdom and to our journey there
except a "caravan"? And what sort of church assumes and exploits
the continuance of this world and of its own cruise in this world
except a "commissary"? The one looks beyond the present to its
transcendent end; the other finds its end within the present.

Browning's distinctive contribution has been to show that these two different orientations foster two entirely different concepts of "faith."

We characterized Gigadibsian faith (true Christian faith) as "radical venture in the face of all risk." This corresponds to what, in a later chapter, Dietrich Bonhoeffer will call "*costly* grace." And the reason the believer is quite willing to face risk and take the cost, is that he has a goal and a priority that far overshadows present benefits and satisfactions, namely, the achievement of the coming kingdom of God. Such faith refers to the end of the world rather than to its continuance.

On the other hand, we characterized Blougramian faith (which actually is nothing more than shrewd calculation) as "figuring the odds so as to minimize all risk." It corresponds to what Bonhoeffer will call "*cheap* grace." Its horizon of reality is confined to the present and to that future which must itself be described as simply a continuance of the present. It expects no more from the future than man himself will be able to create out of present possibilities. But because it is confined within such a horizon, this faith cannot have any other purpose or goal than the reaping of present benefits.

There is another important distinction between these two "faiths" which may not be inherent in the concepts themselves but which certainly is involved as soon as Christianity is introduced. Gigadibsian faith is fundamentally a person-to-person relationship — commitment to and trust in Another. The believer can willingly caravan into a risky future over which he has no control, only because he is following a Leader-Lord whom he knows and trusts, and because he has placed himself in the hands of a loving God.

Blougramian calculation, on the other hand, can never constitute a true person-to-person relationship even if the "believer" does profess the existence of God and Christ. Being interested in another person because of what he can do for you, forming a relationship for what you can get out of it, is nothing truly personal. It is to treat the other as an *object* and not as a person. Indeed, with Bishop Blougram, although it is plain that *belief* in God (or at least the *reputation* of belief in God) is crucial to his "faith," nevertheless, it is questionable whether the existence or nonexistence of God would affect that "faith" one way or another. (And, we might note, the same could be said for some modern theologians.)

But now that we have the distinction, where do we go with it?

In order to make his point, Browning had to present an exceptionally blatant and crass example, yet I am ready to suggest that our churches are full of Blougrams. The difference may be that these people are not as honest in stating their faith as Blougram was — or more likely, that they do not have his self-knowledge in recognizing their faith for what it is. To this extent, they may be more innocent than he was — though it may be that the word should be spelled "n-a-i-v-e."

In any case, how many contemporary Christians have accepted Christ as Lord and Savior without having given any thought to making sacrifices for his sake, to venturing with him in the face of all risk, to dying with him? The extent of their interest and the result of their calculation is that he is the *answer*. He is the miracle worker. He is the source of both material and spiritual blessings. Christ exists only to make life in this world as comfortable and as satisfying as possible, and to guarantee glory in the next world.

And how many contemporary Christians have become members of churches without any serious thought of serving the church or God in and through his church, but simply because a particular congregation holds the promise of providing an interesting group of people with whom to identify, of presenting interesting and exciting programs, of offering various services to assist their efforts in becoming beautiful persons? By what rationale should such motivations be identified as "Christian faith" rather than "Blougramian calculation"?

Now, of course, the church itself bears some responsibility for this state of affairs because it proclaims the gospel of cheap grace and seeks to attract members by catering to their Blougramian self-interests. Yet it is not at this level where I have my deepest concern (nor are we being most germane to the topic of this book). The sadder situation is that *the church itself* plays the Blougram more thoroughly and more blatantly than individual Christians do. Blougram provides a better picture of *the church* than of any individual or group of individuals within the church. Individuals are actually very amateurish in calculating how to play Christianity to their own advantage; congregations do it professionally and scientifically.

The church (and by that, of course, I always mean "by and large," not "totally") understands itself to be a "commissary," and a commissary, we have said, is essentially an *institution.* Just how much of the church's effort and emphasis is directed toward ensuring its institutional success in the world — at perpetuating its quantification, efficacy, power, influence, and popularity? Not only do its strategies *assume* the continuance of the world, it has committed its own institutional existence to the continuance of that world, as being part and parcel of it.

This, indeed, is what the church-growth movement is all about: *sociological* calculations as sharp as those of Blougram though much more scientific — calculations regarding organization, management, marketing, advertising, public relations, propaganda, and so forth — and all of it directed precisely at working the angles, figuring the odds, and minimizing the risks so as to ensure the church's institutional success.

But enough of this. I am already into the next chapter where we will pursue this argument at greater length. However, before moving to that chapter, allow me to interject an important thought that needs to stand as a qualifier both of what has been said in this chapter and what will be said in the next.

My purpose has not been to deny the legitimacy of any and all efforts at church growth, any more than I would deny that accepting Jesus *does* bring personal blessings or that it is proper for church membership to afford particular social satisfactions. I would not try to deny the truth of *everything* Bishop Blougram had to say.

No, even if the church were the very caravan God has called it to be, it would still be also an institution. Even if its eyes were fixed on the end of the world, it still has to live for the present within the continuance of the world. As Blumhardt himself said, "For the time being we must do the best we can with what we have" — which implies the appropriateness of an interest and concern in the church's institutional well-being.

The key to the matter, then, lies in a statement of Jesus': "Set your mind on God's kingdom and his justice before everything else, and all the rest will come to you as well" (Mt. 6:33). Now Scripture nowhere so much as hints that the kingdom is to come through the institutional triumph of the church. In fact, the book of Revelation (particularly in chapter 11) leads up to the coming of Jesus and the achievement of the kingdom by recounting the church's martyr-death and its resurrection by God. Thus, the pursuit of institutional success can in no way be identified as setting your mind on God's kingdom. Such success, then, *must* belong to the other side of the equation, an item from among the "all the rest" which, according to God's good pleasure, may or may not come to you as well.

The one *command* for the caravan church is to seek God's kingdom; the rest you are simply to let come as it will. There is no telling what all may come to the church as well: perhaps sharp sociological calculations, church growth, bishop's robes, and institutional success. But once the church begins to seek these *first,* it becomes Blougramite.

THREE

Success or Fidelity

If, as we have proposed, it is the case that the original, fresh-wineskins church of the New Testament was a *caravan* constituted of *barbershopping expediti,* and if it is the case that the church has become, instead, a *commissary* performing as an *avant-garde Royal Vienna String Quartet,* what motivated that shift, *why* did the church decide to trade in the one set of models for the other? The church saw that the switch would ensure its *success.* It would rather switch than blight.

Our pair of terms this time is "success/fidelity." We use "success" in the way the word is regularly used — applying the measures that would be used in evaluating any organization. Success is determined by the statistics regarding such things as membership, attendance, giving, budget, staff, facilities, and activities. Success equals the number of participants multiplied by the degree of their satisfaction and support. Success, then, is directly dependent upon what might be called "technique-efficiency"— the shrewd calculation and application of sociological principles. "Fidelity," on the other hand, is faithfulness to the gospel, conformity to the mind of Christ, being what the biblical revelation calls the church to be.

Normally, I would guess, the church thinks of success as the product, the consequence, and the payoff of fidelity. Indeed, success is often taken as the *proof* of fidelity. "Look how we are succeeding; we must be doing right. Praise the Lord; see how he is blessing our efforts!"

But this is not the case! Biblically and theologically the two do and must represent a *choice* rather than a *correlation*. A congregation must choose one as its goal. The two are not so nearly alike or so intimately connected that *one* choice can include *both*. No, if the congregations chooses success *over* fidelity, then that choice is itself infidelity, an act of unfaithfulness. If, on the other hand, the congregation chooses fidelity *over* success, success may follow *or it may not* — there is no guarantee, no promise, no assurance, and no connection. Success can and does come to churches that are completely unfaithful, and success can be created through factors that have nothing to do with fidelity.

Ours, we contend, is the *biblical* understanding, seen most clearly, perhaps, in the book of Revelation where the heavenly Christ evaluates the seven congregations of Asia Minor. What is plain throughout is that fidelity is Christ's one and only standard of measurement; no other factors even come into consideration. Of the seven churches, two receive "A's" (unqualified commendation), two receive "F's" (unqualified condemnation), and the rest are scattered between. Of four of the seven churches, we get at least some hint of the outward situation: two are poor, weak, and unsuccessful; and two are lively, rich, and reputable. And would you believe it, the two poor, weak ones receive the "A's" and the two rich, reputable ones receive the "F's"! Jesus apparently got things all backwards.

Clearly, something is going on here to which we need to give attention, for Jesus is speaking deliberately and not accidentally. To one of the "A" churches, Smyrna (Rev. 2:8-11), he says:

> I know your tribulation and your poverty (but you are rich). . . .
> Do not fear what you are about to suffer. . . . Be faithful unto
> death, and I will give you the crown of life.

In other words, your lack of "success" is beside the point; you are rich in fidelity, which is the only thing that counts. There is not even the promise that you *will become* successful; more suffering is all I can offer. But if you will be faithful unto *death* (some prospect that!), I will give you the crown of *life*.

To the other "A" church, Philadelphia (3:7-13), Jesus says:

> Behold, I have set before you an open door, which no one is able to
> shut; I know that you have but little power, and yet you have kept

> *my word and have not denied my name. . . . Because you have
> kept my word of patient endurance, I will keep you from the hour
> of trial which is coming on the whole world.*

The open door is, of course, a door to life and witness; there is no
suggestion that it is a door to success.

To the "F" church of Sardis (3:1-6), the word is:

> *You have the name of being alive, and you are dead. Awake, and
> strengthen what remains and is on the point of death, for I have not
> found your works perfect in the sight of my God. . . . If you will
> not awake, I will come like a thief, and you will not know at what
> hour I will come upon you.*

All the "success indicators" that we normally take as signs of a
church's being alive may not indicate anything of the sort in the
eyes of Jesus.

Finally, to the "F" church of Laodicea (3:14-22) come the
harshest words of all:

> *You are neither hot nor cold. Would that you were cold or hot! So,
> because you are lukewarm, and neither cold nor hot, I will spew
> you out of my mouth. For you say, I am rich, I have prospered,
> and I need nothing; not knowing that you are wretched, pitiable,
> poor, blind, and naked. . . . Those whom I love, I reprove and
> chasten; so be zealous and repent.*

A church's estimate of itself and its estimate in the eyes of the
world (rich, prosperous, needing nothing) may be the exact opposite of Jesus' estimate (wretched, pitiable, poor, blind, and naked).

Now we need to be careful not to push these passages too far
and create a correlation that is simply the reverse of the usual one.
It certainly cannot be taken that a congregation's being small and
weak is *proof* of its fidelity. Obviously, a small, weak congregation
can be wanting and seeking success just as much as a church that
has attained it. No, to *choose* success, to *value* success, to take
success as a measure of worth, are actions that bring Jesus' condemnation. But the fact that success happens to come or not to
come to a church says nothing about its fidelity one way or the
other. The measure of fidelity must be an entirely separate matter.
Fidelity must be measured in terms of obedience to Jesus according
to New Testament standards.

Not only these two chapters of Revelation but also the remainder of the New Testament would point to such a conclusion. For instance, in writing to his congregations, Paul shows no concern as to how they are succeeding, gives them no counsel as to how they might become successful. Fidelity is his one and only interest.

In the previous chapter we started in on the church growth movement, and now we will resume that discussion by putting it up against the New Testament norms.

The movement itself, of course, is much broader than simply the Institute of American Church Growth and its director, Dr. Win Arn; yet those can and do stand as representative of the movement as a whole. At the outset, in unqualified approval and praise, I want to testify that this group has accomplished the best sociological analysis of church growth ever. Using solid scientific studies, they know what makes churches grow and can tell you how to go about achieving institutional success. It is only when they proceed to give *theological* significance to their *sociological* expertise that gross confusions arise.

At the heart of the matter is one of Arn's favorite formulas: "If you will do this and this and this, then God will give the growth." That, if I may say so, is not quite the equivalent of Jesus', "Upon this rock I will build my church; and the gates of hell shall not prevail against it" (Mt. 16:18). Jesus is voicing God's promise that, through his own means, he will preserve a faithful remnant even when the church is in a bad way. Arn is speaking of something else — and trying to have it two ways at once.

If Arn's formula were even to come close to being Christian, the "this and this and this" would have to amount to "seeking first the kingdom of God." Yet even then, Matthew 6:33 should never be taken as a guarantee that if you seek first the kingdom, God will give you *any specified item* out of the "all the rest." That would reduce the God/man relationship to a business deal. If it is truly God's decision and grace that gives the growth, then our doing "this and this and this" has nothing to do with the matter — unless, of course, you are interested in developing a doctrine of works-righteousness. However, if it is the case (as obviously it is) that the "this and this and this" are well-calculated techniques, then the consequent growth is purely and simply the sociological resultant of technique-efficiency (which God may or may not

approve; he didn't appear too happy with the success of the Laodi-
cean church).

The giveaway is the fact that if Arn's "this and this and this"
were slightly reworded, it would work as well for the Ku Klux Klan
as for a church. Yet, if the church does it, God is providing the
growth; if the Klan does it, the Klan is creating its own growth. In
this way, the Klan comes off as the superior outfit, because it does
not have to depend upon outside help for its success.

I once read a piece in which a very successful pastor told how
his people had had the faith that God would fill the church if they
would build an oversized church building. Sure enough, God filled
it! But, baloney (if I may say so in a kindly way)! Where is the
evidence that God cares a snap about what size churches people
build? This congregation's "faith" is the same as that of the de-
velopers who decided that if they would build an oversized mall at a
particular location with the right kind of shops, it would soon be
filled with customers — which it was! This is not *faith*; it is just
smart calculation. And the fact that the pastor who engineered it is
the one who also volunteers to tell us how pleased God was with
the whole venture gives the item a strong Blougramian flavor. Now
for all I know, this congregation may indeed be one that is pleasing
in God's sight. My point is that the evidence we have been given
says nothing one way or another about its fidelity to Jesus Christ
and his vision of the church. That a church is growing is, in itself,
not necessarily an indication of God's approval.

It is time to go, then, to the underside of the church and look
at the church growth movement from there. The Institute of
American Church Growth categorizes one sort of congregation as
"terminally ill." This means that there are congregations in which
sociological factors are so aligned that no techniques can be calcu-
lated to turn the situation around and bring them growth. So be it;
that is a sociological judgment, and the Institute is the best for
making such judgments. But be careful — that category might very
likely have fit the congregations of Smyrna and Philadelphia, the
very ones to which Christ gave "A's." Do we really want to be in
the position of diagnosing as ill what Christ diagnoses as well? I am
not arguing at all with the accuracy of the Institute's sociological
judgment. I am distressed at the evaluational implications that
attend it.

Two observations: In the first place, I am continually amazed at how long many terminally ill congregations are able to continue serving their people and making their faithful witness. The sociological judgment may be correct that they cannot grow, but they do manage to survive in defiance of all sociology. (Perhaps here, where sociological factors are opposing rather than helping, is where we should be the more ready to speak of God's preserving his church. It would seem so in the cases of Smyrna and Philadelphia, at any rate.) If all the terminally ill congregations in our land were suddenly to disappear, the body of Christ would be much the poorer.

Second, at least regarding churches, it seems plain that a congregation can die without ever having been ill in any Christian sense. "Greater love has no one than this, that one lay down his life for his friends" (Jn. 15:13). As we noted earlier, the book of Revelation suggests that the coming of the kingdom involves the whole church "laying down its life" even as its Lord laid down his life. It is this same Lord's will that some of his faithful congregations lay down their lives now. But it is sad when these congregations must also endure the judgment of their peers (which include the F-graded Sardises and Laodiceas) that they are terminally *ill.*

To my mind, the greatest flaw in the church growth movement is its use of *sociological* fact as a thermometer for measuring *Christian* health. In the process, calculation is valued as faith and success is valued as fidelity, and the church is pointed more strongly toward the continuance of the world than toward its end.

But it is dangerous when congregations are encouraged to justify themselves on the grounds of being sociologically fortunate or having the sociological intelligence to achieve worldly success rather than being led to examine themselves according to Christ's standards. ("You say, 'I am rich, I have prospered, and I need nothing'; not knowing that you are wretched. . . .")

"But," you might say, "the fact that a church is growing surely indicates that it is meeting people's needs!" Granted — but just so the circulation figures of *Playboy* magazine prove that it is meeting people's needs. Churchly success is no proof that a congregation is meeting the particular needs for which the gospel is designed or upon which the church is called to concentrate. No, it must be obvious that an organization can be very successful while being spiritually anemic or downright heretical. The implication that fat and happy churches must be good churches reflects the same logic that makes Blougram a great man of faith because he is a bishop who professes to believe everything.

Also, it is too bad that small congregations are made to feel like failures smply because they lack the sociology that produces nice statistics. I confess that I did not respond positively to the IACG movie that starred a number of Southern California "super-churches" and their well-publicized pastors, showing and telling what good pastors and churches should look like. I resent the implication that their model is what we should all want and try to achieve. I know too many pastors and churches that are just as great and just as truly in the will of God that do not follow the Garden Grove Community or Hollywood Presbyterian model at all.

I think it is wrong to hype up congregations with the assurance that "if you do this and this and this, God will give the growth." Certainly that might move some (even many) congregations to do "this and this and this," and they might very well experience growth. But it also sets the stage for some rather traumatic comedowns and disillusionments — both for those congregations that do not have the resources to do "this and this and this," and those that do have the resources but run into sociological roadblocks that prevent the growth formula from working. For them, there is only one conclusion to be drawn: "God doesn't love us; he refused to come through."

Finally, it is not good if church growth is given such overriding priority that a congregation is led to compromise its understanding of the gospel, dilute its witness, or stoop to unworthy devices in the effort to make sales. And do not think that it cannot happen; cheap grace definitely has some marketing advantages over costly grace.

Now we need to look at some of the rationale behind church growth. Examining this will get us back to more specifically biblical considerations.

"Yes; but the church growth movement is derived directly from the New Testament experience and model."

Well, maybe.

"But the New Testament certainly shows an interest in the church growing. God *wants* his church to grow."

True, though the sort of growth the New Testament primarily discusses is described in 2 Peter 3:18: "Grow in the grace and knowledge of our Lord and Savior Jesus Christ." All of the epistles addressed to congregations and congregational leaders (including the seven churches in Revelation) inquire and counsel constantly about this sort of growth; none shows any interest in the congregation's numerical status. The church growth movement shows its interest just as strongly the other way — and has to. Spiritual growth simply is not amenable to sociological statisticizing, scientific analysis, and technique-efficiency — though these are the very things that constitute the church growth movement's strong points. The error is in assuming that these two sorts of growth are necessary correlates. The New Testament puts spiritual growth on the "seek ye first" side of the equation and numerical growth on the "let all the rest come to you as well" side. The church growth movement tends to reverse those poles.

"But the New Testament church *was* growing numerically — and obviously from working at it."

Yes, although it also needs to be said that there is no evidence that the strategy was to grow by creating large, professionalized, technique-effective congregations. The early church was using "caravan" methods for growing a caravan church; we are using "commissary" methods for growing a commissary church. The New Testament certainly cannot be used as a charter for *that!*

"But the New Testament is full of commands to go, teach, preach, tell, proclaim, witness, make disciples, etc. (let's call the package 'evangelism' — sharing the good news), and all of these add up to 'grow.'"

You are right: the New Testament is *overflowing* with such commands. But I dispute that these add up to "grow." Sometimes, of course, they do, but in at least one notable example they added up to "getting yourself crucified and your disciples scattered," with the definite prediction that this could and would happen again and again and again. Paul knew: "I planted, Apollos watered, but God gave the growth" (1 Cor. 3:5). The *growth* is God's business, not ours, and it is a gift according to his choosing, not a guaranteed result for our efforts.

The church *is* commanded to teach, preach, and proclaim the gospel; it is never commanded to "grow." All these other things lie within our range of choice; "growth" does not — it is too much at the mercy of factors beyond our control. Jesus did not chastise any of the Revelation churches for their smallness. The goal and end of our action lies simply in performing our evangelistic tasks faithfully. Are we going where God wants us to go? Are we truly preaching the gospel with which we have been entrusted? In making disciples, do we share Jesus' understanding of discipleship? The church is only responsible for these things; any *results* are up to God.

But if the command becomes simply, "Grow!" our responsibility likewise shifts over to the doing of evangelism *efficiently* rather than *faithfully*. We become concerned only with making things work, with results. We go where we have the best chance of winning converts. We preach only that which people find attractive. We adapt our definition of "disciple" to what people are most willing to be made into. We have to act by calculation, because unless we achieve success, we are being *unfaithful*. But that is a bind God has never put us into: forcing us to desert fidelity with a demand that we produce success.

The one and only test, then, is whether we are doing our evangelistic tasks *faithfully*. That a congregation is in fact growing is no proof that it is doing its tasks *faithfully*; we have already implied that doing them *unfaithfully* might increase the chance of success. Likewise, the fact that a congregation is not growing is no proof that it is not doing its tasks faithfully; there are any number of outside factors that could be prohibiting results. But, by moving the focus away from the New Testament's *theological* category (i.e., our *faithfulness* in evangelistic endeavors) to a *sociological* one (i.e., the *effectiveness* of this sort of endeavor), the church growth movement has confused the biblical understanding of church growth in the very process of appropriating it.

My personal conclusion regarding the church growth movement brings us back to the qualifier that closed our previous chapter. If sociology can be kept in its place and not be allowed to pose as theology, then there definitely is a place in the church for the movement's competent sociology. But this means that growth cannot be a measure of Christian health, calculation cannot pose as faith, and success cannot be an indicator of fidelity. Above all, growth cannot move from "let come to you" to "seek ye first," nor our eyes from the end of the world to its continuance.

We have not said very many positive things about success, but what's wrong with it? Why must it be seen in opposition to fidelity? Why is it a threat to fidelity?

Before we tackle these questions, there is a prior one that must be addressed: What is it that makes a church successful? What does a successful church have that a less successful one does not? I've struggled with this question; and the best way I can think of putting it is that the successful church attracts people and support because it has "class." The term is necessarily vague; but it involves such things as social prestige, taste, and a flair that catches attention. It involves being chic and up-to-date, making people feel that membership enhances their own social standing.

Now it is important to realize that class inevitably will mean different things for different constituencies. For example, many people would deny that class is a concept that can apply to country music in any sense. And yet those who appreciate country music would have very strong convictions about which country music has class and which does not. Class cannot be specified until the constituency itself is specified. This is what I understand the Institute of American Church Growth to be saying in its observation that a growing church customarily is *homogenous,* namely, that it has its constituency defined and knows what it takes to cater to it.

I am familiar with a situation in which there exist, in one town, two congregations of the same denomination, each of which is in equally good standing with the denomination. The first of these is large, professional, and successful. The second is amateurish and struggling. Because there are certain church institutions in the area, many leading families of the denomination (including at least twenty ordained ministers) have moved into town during the decade that the two congregations have existed side by side. One hundred percent of these have joined the large church — almost all of them without even having *visited* the other congregation before making their choice. Why? The one factor that completely swings the balance is that the large church has class, and the small one does not.

My observations, of course, have not been confined to just this one situation where the matter seems so clear, but my conclusions are as follows. Most people probably find themselves in the congregation they do because it is the local representative of the denomination in which they were reared, although denominational loyalty is no longer as strong a factor as it used to be. But where it is a matter of open choice, is it or is it not the case that class (according to what class means for the respective individual) is the deciding factor?

Perhaps by using the word "class," I am simply trying to capture the mood that pervades our earlier three concepts of commissary, avant-garde, and Royal Vienna String Quartet. In any case, class is the key to success. This is not to say that success never comes to a church without class. Neither is it to say that class is the only factor ever involved in success. Nevertheless, for a church to have class is its best assurance of success. Look around you; identify those congregations that would have to be rated most successful, and see whether, in the eyes of their own constituencies, they do not display class.

"OK, you're right," you might reply, "but what's wrong with that? What difference does it make what attracts people, or what means are used to get people interested and into church, as long as we give them the gospel after getting them there? We even can find Scripture on the matter: Paul's seeking to please all men in all things that they may be saved (1 Cor. 10:33), and his taking every thought captive to the obedience of Christ (2 Cor. 10:5)."

Yes, there are those Scriptures — although we must give full weight to the phrase "that they may be *saved*" and full consideration to the thought's being made captive to Christ rather than Christ being made captive to the thought. And this brings us to the heart of our argument. It has to do with the issue of means, an issue almost totally ignored by the church. The common assumption is that if one's goal is good and if the chosen goal means success, then everything is as it should be. Yet this is to overlook all the truth of Marshall McLuhan's dictum that the medium *is* the message.

We assume, rather, that means are in themselves neutral. So our wisdom dictates that we look around and find a means, a technique of organization, programming, advertising, and public relations that the world has shown to be effective.

"We're going to score a lot of touchdowns, we're on a winning team. . . . This is the Lord's picture, and he does not sponsor any flops," as the executive producer of the Charles Colson

Born Again movie was quoted. If smart, classy Christians undertake a project, they can claim the Lord's sponsorship, and that is a sure guarantee of success. Does this movie producer not recall the people God sponsored in history — Israel, a born loser among the nations? Does the producer not know that the high point of the Old Testament is the picture of the Suffering Servant who was "despised and rejected by men"? Does this producer think that Jesus' being deserted by his followers and executed as a criminal indicates that he was a success in the world? Has he not heard that Paul called himself and his fellow Christians "the scum of the world, the dregs of all things"? Does the producer not know which of the churches of Asia Minor Jesus admitted to sponsoring? Does he actually think that God is committed to ensuring the box office success of his or any other movie?

No, in our lust for success we overlook the fact that it takes two different conditions to make techniques right. Not only must the technique be an effective one in and of itself, it must also be *appropriate* to the content it is intended to promote. It is when the medium and the message are consonant with one another — and only then — that things are as they should be. The medium and the message must be right for each other.

What so often happens in the church's experience is that a technique of worldly effectiveness looks good and is adopted. And then, because success is the only consideration (techniques have no other purpose), the gospel message is subtly pruned, shaped, and contorted until it fits the technique. "Please all men in all things," yes; but if the gospel is falsified in the process, men will not be saved. It is quite possible for Christ to be taken captive by a technique rather than the technique being taken captive for Christ.

Now we shall turn to some examples. If the gospel is proclaimed in a setting and by media that all communicate gentility, graciousness, and sedate propriety (luxurious appointments, sonorous music, cultured rhetoric, dignified behavior), will that gospel be heard as the scandal, the offense, the folly, the humility, and the stumbling-stone of which the Scripture speaks? Can the Suffering Servant of God, the Son of Man who had no place to lay his head, the humble preacher of Galilee, truly be made present by such means in such a setting? Can one speak of nonconformity to the world in a setting that radiates worldly respectability?

Or consider the popular, contemporary phenomenon of gospel rock. The assumption clearly is that rock music itself, as a medium, is neutral, the message lying entirely in the lyrics. Thus, if one takes either the actual music or the style of secular rock and gives it Christian lyrics, the performance becomes a Christian activity, that is, worship and the proclamation of the gospel.

However, that assumption must be strongly questioned. And the success of the technique in its satisfying the customers ought not to be taken as a proof of Christian validity; success is not the guarantee of fidelity. The *music* of rock is just as much a cultural expression as are its *lyrics*. And what is (or was) the nature of the culture that created the rock idiom as its expression? Most conspicuously, it was oriented around alcohol, drugs, and sex. The lyrics themselves testify to this. Woodstock was the most graphic demonstration of rock's home and context. Is it correct, then, that the musical idiom itself bears no touch of all this, or is it the case that the music itself was meant as an expression of the same orgasmic "high" for which alcohol, drugs, and sex have been valued?

Furthermore, the rock generation was also very much disillusioned, without faith in society's traditional values, without any sense of order or structure in life. And does not its musical idiom express the same chaos, absurdity, and lostness? And does this, then, become an appropriate vehicle for affirming a gospel that centers upon the loving lordship, purpose, and plan of God?

Again, the rock generation was very self-centered. By that I mean the horizon of one's sense of reality and significance was constricted pretty much to that of personal experience — what *I* am feeling, what is happening to *me*, what is going on within *me*, — that is about as far as my concern and interest go. Listen to the rock lyrics and see if this is not the philosophy they reflect. Then check out the lyrics of gospel rock and see if they do not have the same orientation. Is not "my personal experience of Jesus," or "what Jesus has done *for me*," the dominating focus of gospel rock lyrics? And can that be an adequate statement of a gospel which, in its biblical setting, speaks so strongly of discipleship and of God's plan for humanity at large?

Finally, I would suggest that the greatest appeal and effect of rock music lies in its emotionalism — emotionalism of such power that the appropriate physical response is sensual, bodily gyration.

There is a distinction between emotion and emotionalism. Emotion is entirely proper and appropriate as the response to a word, a message, or a situation that is poignant. Emotionalism, on the other hand, is emotion that is artificially generated through studied techniques (loud sound, frenzy, very strong beat) for the sake of the emotion itself and not for the sake of communicating any particular message. It may very well be that the emotionalism of rock was valued primarily as a means of blotting out the sense of life's lostness and absurdity which we commented on earlier.

Perhaps the closest thing the Bible gives us to a description of a rock concert is from 1 Kings 18:25-29:

> Then Elijah said to the prophets of Baal, "Choose one of the bulls and offer it first, for there are more of you; invoke your god by name, but do not set fire to the wood." So they took the bull provided for them and offered it, and they invoked Baal by name from morning until noon, crying, "Baal, Baal, answer us"; but there was no sound, no answer. They danced wildly beside the altar they had set up. At mid-day Elijah mocked them: "Call louder, for he is a god; it may be he is deep in thought, or engaged, or on a journey; or he may have gone to sleep and must be woken up." They cried still louder and, as was their custom, gashed themselves with swords and spears until the blood ran. All afternoon they raved and ranted till the hour of the regular sacrifice, but still there was no sound, no answer, no sign of attention.

When it was Elijah's turn to call upon the *true* God, how shortsighted and faithless he would have been if he had adopted the same *methods* of worship as the Baal prophets. Such methods would have suggested that Yahweh was little more than a superior Baal. And do we want to suggest that the message of rock is close enough to that of the gospel that the only change required is some mention of the name Jesus? Certainly, the gospel, with its abundance of the extraordinary, warrants an appropriately extraordinary medium to accentuate the extraordinariness of its message. Does rock music qualify as this medium?

I am not at all arguing that it is wrong for those who do to listen to rock music and enjoy it. I am denying that a mere change in lyrics immediately "Christianizes" that enjoyment, transforming it into an experience of worship and a hearing of the gospel.

Also, I am not adverse to having someone convince me of an instance where rock music has been sufficiently transformed and redeemed to be a true communicator of the full gospel message. Of course, I will not agree that simply because the music attracted people and that some of them "accepted Christ" amounts to an instance of true communication, but I can see the theoretical possibility of a rock production being the vehicle for a faithful rendition of the gospel. Yet this would not at all change the one point I want to make. My objection is to the easy assumption that our choice of means or media has no effect on the gospel to which we witness. I object to the assumption that, if the means works, that in itself is proof enough that our action has been a faithful one. Thus, wherever you come out regarding rock music, at least admit that there are issues involved that call for careful consideration and profound discernment.

Our final example is from the recent Here's-Life-America ("I Found It") campaign. This was conceived by an advertising man, and, in a television interview, he cited the biblical account of the day of Pentecost (the Holy Spirit doing a media blitz on the city of Jerusalem) as his inspiration and precedent.

I have two difficulties with this. For one thing, in the process of latching on to one very exceptional instance of mass conversion (which the New Testament itself accentuates as being exceptional if not absolutely unique), he has deliberately overlooked the countless instances and evidences that establish normative New Testament evangelism as being very much of a personalized, face-to-face approach. Such picking and choosing is not a good way to let the Bible speak.

My second difficulty is that the parallel between his campaign and Pentecost holds only to the extent that both were efforts which resulted in mass conversions in the name of Jesus. But the man totally overlooks the complete discrepancy of the *means* employed. I do not know whether the Holy Spirit even ought to be called a means, but it is quite evident that nothing remotely resembling modern advertising methods were involved at Pentecost. Again, his is a way of saying that the medium has nothing to do with the message, that there is no reason to raise the question of means, and that the only consideration is whether one achieves success.

How consonant were the means of the Here's-Life-America campaign with the message it was to serve? The heart of the campaign centered on mass telephoning, a technique that has proved very successful in certain types of merchandising. But what particular types of merchandising? When my phone rings and I find myself getting a stock line from someone I do not know and who does not know me — or when, on the basis of some sort of vague promise of a prize, I am inveigled into phoning a number where I get a stock line from someone I do not know and who does not know me — I can draw a fairly accurate conclusion about what is being sold. It is usually some flashy but tawdry bit of junk, the profit on which must be made by convincing masses of people that they can get something pretty nice without much cash outlay.

Quality merchandise is not sold in this manner (it doesn't have to be). If it is really good and represents a major investment, the seller will simply offer it and let the interest of the buyer bring him to examine it. Both the buyer and the seller will want to meet each other and learn enough about each other to judge whether the product is right for the buyer's needs. Both buyer and seller are interested in the buyer's knowing the full truth about the product before he buys. And what, inevitably, does it say about Jesus when he is made the object of the first, rather than the second, method of salesmanship?

Further, "I Found It" is an example of the sales gimmick (undoubtedly of proven effectiveness) that seeks to engage the customer and catch his interest while declining to tell him what is being sold. It is like the encyclopedia salesman who gets into the house by insisting that he is conducting a survey, and hiding, for as long as possible, the fact that he also is selling books. Such an approach betrays a lack of respect for the customer (the truth is withheld from him), and a lack of faith in the product (the salesman is fearful that the customer will lose interest once he finds out what he is selling). Again, quality merchandise is not sold in this manner; the product is introduced at the outset, in the conviction that it is its own best selling point.

Finally, there is the sales ploy of refusing to name the price until the very end of the pitch, getting the buyer to guess a price higher than the actual price, starting with a high price and then offering the buyer discounts, and so forth. It is all too evident that

Here's-Life-America (along with most of our evangelism programs) showed no urgency in getting around to talk about the *cost* of being a Christian, the *price* of following Jesus. In fact, we are dishonest enough to allow and even encourage people to accept Jesus with the impression that no cost is involved. It was not so when Jesus himself was recruiting disciples. Evidence indicates that his approach did not begin with or center upon promises of blessings for those who accepted him. He simply said, "Come, follow me" (a rather demanding challenge in itself), with no holding back on what that would likely involve. He even told the parable about counting the cost *before* undertaking a venture (Lk. 14:25-33). Of course, it can be argued that this approach will not bring many sales, but perhaps it is the case that Jesus is not as caught up in the eagerness for making sales as Here's-Life-America.

It was Dietrich Bonhoeffer who developed the crucial distinction between cheap grace and costly grace:

> Cheap grace is the deadly enemy of our church. We are fighting today for costly grace. . . . The essence of grace, we suppose, is that the account has been paid in advance; and, because it has been paid, everything can be had for nothing.
> . . . Cheap grace means grace as a doctrine, a principle, a system. It means forgiveness of sins proclaimed as a general truth. . . . Cheap grace means the justification of sin without the justification of the sinner. Grace alone does everything, they say, and so everything can remain as it was before. . . . Instead of following Christ, let the Christian enjoy the consolations of his grace! . . . Cheap grace is the grace we bestow on ourselves. Cheap grace is the preaching of forgiveness without requiring repentance, baptism without church discipline, communion without confession, absolution without personal confession. Cheap grace is grace without discipleship, grace without the cross, grace without Jesus Christ, living and incarnate.
>
> Costly grace is the gospel which must be *sought* again and again, the gift which must be *asked* for, the door at which a man must *knock.* Such grace is *costly* because it calls us to follow, and it is grace because it calls us to follow *Jesus Christ.* It is costly because it costs a man his life, and it is grace because it gives a man the only true life. It is costly because it

condemns sin, and grace because it justifies the sinner. Above all, it is *costly* because it cost God the life of his Son . . . and what has cost God much cannot be cheap for us.[2]

What we have been discussing in this chapter simply carries Bonhoeffer's thought one step further. It is altogether right and even necessary that the church find and use different media (means) for expressing and communicating the gospel, for without a medium there is no way of proclaiming any message. Nothing we have said is in opposition to the use of means; we have opposed only the *indiscriminate, unexamined selection* of means.

As long as a church's sole focus and priority is fidelity, there is no problem. The test, then, always is: Is this means consonant with the gospel of costly grace it would serve? Is the medium speaking with the message or against it? Congruence, here, *is* fidelity; and whether or not success attends the effort is entirely in the hands of God, the God who has never shown a great deal of interest in success one way or the other.

But once success is allowed to become a church's goal and interest, watch out! For one thing, there will be the attempt to imitate the world's ways of achieving class. After all, the world is the admitted expert at devising techniques that spell success. Further, the worldly media inevitably operate from the premise that the way to success is to pander to people's fancies and desires (what they call their *needs*), at bargain rates, at as little cost to and demand upon them as possible. None of these means, then — the social advantages of gentility and culture, the tremendous popularity of rock, or the proven efficiency of modern advertising methods — is particularly suited to the message of costly grace that calls us to follow, costs us our lives, condemns sin, and required the life of God's own Son. However, these means *will* work very well — *do* work very well — in relation to cheap grace. And the church finds itself blessed with success *in promoting cheap grace.*

It is left for you to decide how much this analysis applies to your own congregation — how dedicated that congregation is to success, how eager it is to display class, how given it is to the use of inappropriate and unworthy means, and the extent to which it has become satisfied with believing in and promoting cheap grace.

[2]*The Cost of Discipleship*, pp. 45-48.

FOUR

How to Be Inviting
Through Body Language

Perhaps my questioning of whether church success is a Christian value has led a number of readers to assume that my view of the church is basically opposed to (or at least cool toward) any great emphasis upon *evangelism*. This chapter is intended to correct that misimpression.

I *am* opposed to "evangelism at all costs," that is, the cost of distorting the gospel in the effort to make it more attractive to the public. This means that I am obligated to come up with an alternative style of evangelism that is appropriate to the caravan church and true to the measure of the New Testament. My proposal is different from what is normally understood to be good evangelistic style. I call it "evangelism through body language."

Body language is one of the psychological discoveries (or fads) of our day. (Like others of its kind, my guess is that it is about ten percent discovery and ninety percent fad.) Proponents of body language claim that, subconsciously, in our conversation with other people, our physical postures are more expressive of our true feelings and communicate on a much deeper level than the words we speak. For example, if, when speaking to someone, I stand with my arms folded, I am actually indicating that I want to hold myself in. I am saying that I basically do not trust the other person enough to open out to him.

Body language analysts claim to be able to read a whole glossary of such signals, and thus to be able to tell a great deal about what *really* is going on between people in conversation. Although we may have here a grain of truth swimming in a bucket of

57

hogwash, body language can provide a means for getting at something very important regarding evangelism.

The body whose language is evangelism is, of course, the one
Paul calls "the body of Christ." And this immediately points us
toward a root distinction to which we will return a bit later,
namely, that rather than being a *delegated* responsibility,
evangelism is a function of the church itself, of the faith community as community, of the body *as* body. Paul best speaks to this
point:

> *Now you are Christ's body, and each of you a limb or organ of it.*
> *Within our community God has appointed, in the first place*
> *apostles, in the second place prophets, thirdly teachers; then*
> *miracle-workers, then those who have gifts of healing, or ability to*
> *help others or power to guide them, or the gift of ecstatic utterance*
> *of various kinds. . . . Put love first; but there are other gifts of the*
> *Spirit at which you should aim also, and above all prophecy.*
> *When a man is using the language of ecstasy he is talking with*
> *God, not with men, for no man understands him; he is no doubt*
> *inspired, but he speaks mysteries. On the other hand, when a man*
> *prophesies, he is talking to men, and his words have power to*
> *build; they stimulate and they encourage. The language of ecstasy*
> *is good for the speaker himself, but it is prophecy that builds up*
> *Christian community. . . . So if the whole congregation is*
> *assembled and all are using the "strange tongues" of ecstasy, and*
> *some uninstructed persons or unbelievers should enter, will they*
> *not think you are mad? But if all are uttering prophecies, the*
> *visitor, when he enters, hears from everyone something that*
> *searches his conscience and brings conviction, and the secrets of*
> *his heart are laid bare. So he will fall down and worship God,*
> *crying, "God is certainly among you!"*
> —1 Cor. 12:27-28; 14:1-4, 23-25

The path of Paul's thought (and the outline for our discussion of it) is as follows: The calling of the church is to function as
the body of Christ. Within the body, the members are to operate,
not for their own enjoyment or enhancement, but to the end that
the body as a whole is built up. When operating in this way, body
language is such that an observer can read it and be moved to fall
down and worship God, crying, "God is certainly among you!"
This is *evangelism*.

It is body language that best wins men to Christ. We need to make a primary point in that regard. Paul never calls the church "the *torso* of Christ," with the head as something different and presumably separable from the torso. No, the body is an inclusive term designating the totality of torso and all the members, including the head. Along with Paul, we should never refer to the church as something apart from Christ; the church is his body only when he is present and included.

And it is this body that is to be the evangelist. This idea runs contrary to the accepted pattern of evangelism which, more often than not, sees evangelization as taking place *apart from* the life of the church; it is only *after* the prospect has been evangelized that he is handed over to the care of a congregation. I am not saying that true evangelism *cannot* take place this way, but this is not the New Testament's normal, preferred mode.

So the evangelist is not a traveling celebrity preacher. The evangelist is not the pastor in the pulpit. The evangelist is not the congregation's evangelism committee. The evangelist is not the laity making house calls. All these may be, can be, and should be members of that body which is doing evangelism, but it is the body itself (including the head) that is the evangelist. The Christian *community* is the body whose language is evangelism.

The purpose and goal of evangelism, after all, is to help people see Jesus, meet Jesus, and know Jesus. And if he is "the head," where else can or should he be seen other than in his body?

The truest and best evangelistic approach is to invite the prospect to come to church. I know this is contrary to the usual evangelistic counsel. Indeed, many instructors would insist that unless you push the prospect to make a personal decision for Christ, you are not evangelizing.

It is widely known how, almost instinctively, lay visitors resist the idea of asking a stranger flat out to accept Jesus Christ as Lord and Savior. And the more I think about it, the more I think that this instinct is correct. This, in effect, is to ask the customer to buy a product sight unseen. Or, to put it more accurately, it is to ask him to marry a head before he even has seen the body of which it is a part. It is asking him to become a "member" — a hand, an ear, or an eye — of a body he has never met.

But simply *talking about* Jesus (even if the talk is good and true) cannot qualify as "body language." It is too superficial in the same sense that some psychologists claim that simply hearing what is said in a conversation is superficial in comparison to the truth revealed by body language. For one thing, these evangelistic words about Jesus tend to be confined to great promises of what Christ will do for you if you only accept him. Body language, conversely, allows you to see what Christ has done and is doing for the members of his body. Furthermore, it also lets you see how members perform and what is *expected* of them under the headship of Christ (which should include the cost factors of grace).

Of course, if the prospect already knows the Christian who approaches him, he already has observed some body language in seeing who that person is and how he conducts himself. Nevertheless, the prospect will have a better chance of seeing Christ in his body if he can witness the members *together*, involved in the full-fledged motions of their body language. In any case, the best evangelism is still the invitation to "Come with me to church!"

Yet there is a difficulty with this approach. Body language will not achieve its purpose if the church to which the prospect is invited is not truly functioning as the body of Christ. If the body is not acting under the direction of its head, the visitor is going to have a hard time guessing that a head is even present.

Here we must pick up a caution from our previous chapter. The fact that body language is working and bringing in people is not necessarily an indication that everything is as it should be. Body language is a *medium*; authentic evangelism has to do with a particular *message*, namely, the Christian gospel. It is quite possible that the body language of a particular church can effectively project an image of success (cheap grace) that attracts people and leads them to join. (We even have opined that success and class more effectively attract the public than the costly-grace gospel.) The soul-winning language of such a church, then, is actually the language of the world and not of the body *of Christ.*

Thus, the authenticity of a congregation's evangelism is not proved one way or another by its growth rate. Authentic evangelism consists in just two factors: (1) the church projecting its true existence and performance as the body of Christ; and (2) the church actively inviting and welcoming people to come, see (both the congregation and Christ in the congregation), and join. But how many people accept the invitation is a matter entirely out of the church's control or responsibility. God no more promises evangelistic "success" than any other kind. It is quite possible that a congregation that is not growing at all may be doing a better and a more faithful job of evangelizing than the congregation that is growing at a great pace. The very word "evangelism" connotes a spread of *the gospel* rather than the growth of *the institutional church*, and these two are not necessarily the same thing.

Let us suggest, then, some of the common postures or ges-tures that do not qualify as true evangelistic body language. First, we do not invite a prospect to church merely so the *preacher* can be the evangelist. (Paul specifically says that "if *all* are uttering prophecies," the visitor will hear something "from *everyone*" that will touch his life.) To center simply on the preacher is only to substitute *pulpit* words for *visit* words, and this is not "body" lan-guage. In this regard, both clergy and laity together need to take care not to behave in a way that suggests that the minister is *the head* of this body. Being won to an attractive pastor or attractive sermons is not the same thing as being won to Christ. If our body language says, "Look at our fine pastor," it cannot be helping people to see Jesus.

Second, if the church's body language says, "See what a fine program we have, how attractive our facilities are, how beautiful our music is, or how many activities you can enjoy," the visitor will not be able to see Jesus.

Finally, we do not invite people to church merely in the hope that they will enjoy the fellowship as a social occasion. This one, we will see, does get closer to true body language, but unless the socializing points beyond itself, it doesn't make Jesus visible. After all, even the world is pretty good at providing opportunities to socialize; the church's must be sociability with a difference.

None of these postures, then, qualifies as evangelistic body language even if they do win people who want to join. No, as Paul suggested, the body of Christ must consist in that sort of activity, which, when observed by a visitor, might convince him that he is in the presence of God. Words alone seldom do that; only true body language will communicate at that level and with that power. But what, specifically, should our visitor see? What are the sights that might bring him to Christian faith?

First, I would suggest, the visitor should see the same thing that impressed observers of the early church, and led them to exclaim, "See how these Christians *love* one another!" Now this "loving one another" cannot be the simple enjoyment of one another's company; it must be Jesus' "as I have loved you" love. It must be something great enough that the visitor will sense the difference and get curious: "Where are they getting *that*? That isn't what I saw at Kiwanis last week or in the tavern last night."

This love must go beyond our feelings about one another and demonstrate how we *care* about one another, how we *share* with one another, what we are willing *to do* for one another. It should be the case, also, that the visitor will see that the "one another" we love is not confined to our own circle of friends but includes all our Christian brothers and sisters, and indeed, all those in need, all those we can serve. Recall, from Acts, chapters 3 and 4, that it was only when Peter and John practiced the loving, caring, and serving body language in healing a lame beggar (who presumably was not a Christian) that the people, knowing Peter and John were uneducated and untrained, began to recognize that they had been with Jesus.

Seeing this love for one another, the visitor would next notice, I hope, that the body got that way because of its *biblical* orientation. Now the body language at this point does not lie simply in noting how many people carry Bibles or how often Scripture is quoted. The visitor must see that the love of these Christians comes from the fact that they have studied the Bible and have let it mold them. A biblical church is not so much one that uses the Bible as it is one that lets the Bible use it. It is a body that studies, loves, and *lives* the Bible.

Finally, through all of this body language, the visitor ought to realize that the entirety of the congregation's life-together is following the Lord and giving him praise. It must consciously and deliberately be made evident that this body includes a head, and that he is the sole source and center of the congregation's being and activity, of all its body language. This language exists to say but one thing, namely, that it is not *our* body but *his*, the very body *of*

Christ. Thus, the visitor is led to see *him* — and that is evangelism.

Now it is not our desire to deny that the other forms and methods more customarily called evangelism have their place. However, that place, we insist, is within the context of a congregation doing its body language; those methods are true only insofar as they subserve this one. A major aspect of Christianity's good news is that Jesus Christ has (or is) a body of which the individual can be a part, a habitation he can call home. It makes sense, therefore, that no full-fledged evangelism can take place in disregard of that body.

In this matter, then, as with the rest, you are left to analyze your own congregation, and to examine the state of its evangelism. What does your congregation communicate through body language? How *inviting* is it, and how well does it *extend* invitations?

FIVE

How a Church Can Give Its People the Business

In this chapter we will talk about the local congregation and its function of conducting "business." We are using this term in the broadest possible sense to include not only those decisions dealing with property, personnel, and what we usually call "business affairs," but all the multitudinous decisions that affect programs, activities, and other aspects of the church.

There are two very different ways to make these decisions, and they correspond rather directly to our commissary and caravan models. In a commissary church, the great majority of important decisions are made by the pastor and professional staff. Many of these decisions are made through regular church channels and with the help of an official board or various committees. Nevertheless, by the time matters get to the congregation they are pretty well accomplished. Most of the time, the people do not expect or want things any other way; they come only to see what "the church" is going to put on for them.

I am not saying that this method is undemocratic; it is democratic in precisely the same way as our political system and most of our organizations are: we elect officials and representatives to make decisions for us, and these officials and representatives are ultimately responsible to us. Yet, for a caravan church, democracy is not good enough; participation and community decision are required. A caravan may have leaders and even committees (i.e., groups with special responsibilities), but in the final analysis each member has an equal investment in the life of the caravan and equal responsibility for its existence and survival. Each individual is as much a part of the church as anyone else. His contribution is as necessary as anyone else's. He does not come to see what the church proposes to put on for him, because he is as much "the church" as anyone else is.

That the New Testament envisions the caravan form of congregational government seems obvious from the way churchly admonishment is directed. In Revelation's letters to the seven churches and in the great majority of the Pauline and general epistles, when the writer calls for something to happen, he addresses the congregation as such and not any staff or official board. Decisions and actions are seen as the responsibility of the community, although this clearly is not taken to mean that all leadership functions are abrogated.

Now it is evident that the larger a congregation is, the more difficult it will be to practice participatory community, and perhaps at this point representative democracy becomes the only practical form of church government. But as we have suggested before, large congregations chose to become such on their own, have created their own problems in regard to the New Testament model, and will have to take responsibility for their own solutions. But one way or another, the people ought to be given the business.

Even so, to talk about the business of the church is to talk also about disagreement, tension, and conflict. As more people participate there will be more ideas as to how things should go, and thus there will be more controversy. So there is no doubt that the larger, commissary-type churches have the easier time of it. The proper people are in charge and the average church-goer is not consulted, his opinion is not welcomed, and he probably does not realize that he has a right to one. The views of a single member — or even a small group of members — are not given serious attention. In the large, professionally-organized church, it takes a major rebellion to endanger the peace. In barbershopping caravans, tempests in teapots are the order of the day.

And the principle holds true not only in regard to conflicts. In the commissary church it simply is not true as John Fawcett's hymn states: "We share our mutual woes; our mutual burdens bear." The private problems of an individual or family do not become those of the church as such. One of the staff professionals takes care of the matter, and most of the church members probably do not even hear of it, let alone become concerned and involved.

Often, the burden to bear is another person — a person, to state it kindly, with many idiosyncrasies. In the commissary church this type of person is easily tolerated, because the most he can do is come and watch the program. In the caravan church this type of person could become a real pain, because, along with everyone else, he must be recognized, lived with, given his part of the action, and (by the grace of God) loved.

So a commissary church is more peaceful than its caravan counterpart, but that is not to say that it is more healthy. Its peace is achieved at the cost of limiting communal participation. We do not mean to say that tension and conflict are good in church life; we do say that it is good for the life of the church that those things are free to appear. And in this sense, the fact that the troubles of the New Testament congregations are so apparent is a sign that they are doing something right. Let us examine what a caravan church should do when disagreements, tensions, conflicts, and fightings arise.

The key lies in another pair of contrasting terms. This pair, however, is completely different from previous pairs because, although it is important to distinguish between them, we are not pushing for an either/or choice; both must be and should be kept in the picture. The two terms are "votables" and "non-votables."

There are some issues in the life of a congregation for which it would be utterly inconceivable to propose that they be settled by voting. For example, the church does not *vote* on whether Jesus is Lord. Issues of this sort could be called "matters of principle," or "constitutive principles"; they represent the commitments that *define* the community and make it what it is. There can be no giving up of these without destroying the community (or at least the *Christianity* of the community) in the process. If and when these issues come into question, I have no good advice on procedures, for you have an irreconcilable fight on your hands. What ought to happen in such a case is for those who are deserting the constitutive principles (their baptismal, ordinational, creedal, or church-membership vows) to be honest enough to recognize that they have moved outside the bounds of the community, and so absent themselves in actuality.

"Votable issues," on the other hand, such as "what hymnal should we use in the church?" are those that can be settled one way or the other (or compromised) without affecting the essential character of the community. These issues ought not be called "trivial" (because most often they are not seen that way), yet certainly, in comparison to the "non-votable" issues, they are trivial. None of them is worth destroying the community over, and at most, they produce unnecessary conflicts.

Now I suppose there may be borderline issues which could be either "votable" or "non-votable"; nevertheless, such issues are likely to be few and far between. But the real secret behind how a caravan church conducts business is to keep everyone aware of the distinction between the two types of issues as well as aware of which type is under consideration at any given time. When this is done, interesting things can begin to happen.

The more unified a group is regarding its "non-votables," the freer it will be to argue over its "votables" in a completely healthy, open, and non-threatening way. The caravan church is more likely to have such a united commitment on "non-votables," simply because its members have been given more opportunities to share and witness, to know just how they stand with one another. On the other hand, where there is any doubt about unity on the "non-votables," there is bound to be touchiness about the "votables" as well. There will always be the hidden agenda, the suspicion that deeper issues are involved.

So it may be that a peaceful commissary is *afraid* to entrust much decision-making to the people for fear that it could lead to deeper issues and consequent disorder. And it may be that a caravan's regular tempests in teapots represent a healthy freedom, a sign that its "non-votables" are in such good shape that it can afford the fun of letting everybody sound off on whatever they feel like sounding off about.

When all understand that a "votable" is a "votable," they may still have strong and genuine feelings on the issue, but the vote itself is tantamount to the consensus by which some communities operate. Contrary to the common understanding, a consensus does not necessarily mean that everyone agrees. It can mean that some members have chosen to go along with the majority in order to keep things moving, and because the matter is not important enough to risk disunity. And just so with the right kind of vote — "win a few, lose a few"; the community is operating as it should whether I get my way or not.

No one would say that barbershop business meetings are the most efficient method of procedure — they are not. But they do accomplish some things that a more structured and efficient organization cannot. In the congregation to which I belong, we have congregational business meeting one long Sunday evening each month — much more frequently than most churches. Very few if any decisions are made without the involvement of the entire body.

A few years ago, a sharp Mennonite family (which may be a redundancy) was looking for a church home. They visited one of our Sunday morning services. They were pleased, and decided to attend one of our evening business meetings in order to learn more about our church. (This was a real switch. Goodness knows it's hard enough to get *members* to come to business meetings, let alone *visitors*.)

The evening was, as usual, a rather wild and spirited affair. Everyone felt free to have his say on everything in the form of passionate and highly-opinionated speeches (except mine, of course). There was also, as usual, a goodly amount of wisecracking and general hee-haw. (One of the best ways of keeping it clear that "votables" are "votables" is by not taking them too seriously.) We made it through the evening — if not the business — and a good time was had by all. The visitors were hooked, eager for their chance to get in on the action.

In that one business meeting, where they saw the congregation with its hair down, and where body language was most visible, they received more insight into the essential nature of the congregation (warts and all) than they would have received if they had attended our Sunday morning services for an entire month. They saw what sort of standing the individual (even the idiosyncratic individual) had within the group, and how these individuals related to one another as a body. They observed the kind of Christian freedom that does not evade or play down disagreements, tensions, and conflicts, but takes them in stride. Above all, the ease with which the group handled "votables" probably was a better indicator of the power and character of its constitutive principles than listening to sermons or reading statements of faith. At least here faith could be seen in action and at work — and that in a situation of potential stress and trial.

The church is at least as much, if not more, the church when it is making its decisions of program, spending, outreach, and service as it is when it is worshiping — particularly if that worship represents the planning of professionals rather than the expression of the people. How is it with your congregation? What do your business procedures say about the nature and health of your faith community? Should your church give its people the business?

SIX

Whose Little Microcosm Are You?

With this chapter we turn away from congregational style to look at the style of the individual Christian. However, that is not as great a change of focus as one might think. Kierkegaard once said, "The individual, in community, is a microcosm which qualitatively reduplicates the macrocosm," and he then quoted a Latin motto from Terence, "To know one is to know all."[3]

With the words "in community," Kierkegaard is applying his observation only to the caravan church. If, with forceps, he is saying, you were to reach into a caravan congregation, catch the first individual (microcosm) that came to you, and examine him under your microscope, you could learn all that is essential about the caravan (macrocosm) itself. Although Kierkegaard stopped here, the Bible would suggest that the principle could be carried a step further. Catch the first Christian congregation (microcosm) that comes your way, and at least in theory, you could discover the nature of the coming kingdom of God (macrocosm).

Kierkegaard, however, was intent to show that the "random specimen" method would not even begin to work with a commissary church. In a caravan, every member shares all the powers and responsibilities and, indeed, the very character of every other member and of the congregation itself. But in the commissary church the picture would be entirely different depending upon whether the investigator happened to catch one of the proprietors

---

[3]Translated and quoted in Vernard Eller, *Kierkegaard and Radical Discipleship*, p. 436.

or one of the customers, one of the performers or one of the spectators, one of the officers who gives the orders or a member of the hoi polloi who takes them. The commissary does not even pretend to be the sort of homogenous community that the caravan aspires to be.

Nevertheless, there is a sense in which Kierkegaard's experiment probably *does* apply to commissaries as well as caravans. The reason we are attracted to a church with class is that we want to be individuals with class. We want a church that enjoys social respectability because, as individuals, we want to be socially accepted. We want a fine building for our church for the same reason we want fine homes for ourselves. We want to be part of a successful church because we are interested in being successful persons. As I have said before, the church is not so dumb; it sees the advantage of giving people what they want, of *being* what the people themselves *are*.

It is almost inevitable, then, that there will be a congruence between our congregational style and our personal style, between what we see as congregational values and what we see as personal values. Notice that this relationship can go either of two ways. It may be that the congregation comes to be what it is because the members are what they are. Or it may be that, being what it is, the congregation encourages and nurtures members in becoming what they do become. My guess is that the relationship works both ways at once, that congregation and people each feed into the other. In any case, talking about individual Christian lifestyle without giving attention to the church community can only get at part of the truth; the congregation is the *context* in which the personal behavior is meant to take place.

The question, then, to which we now address ourselves is: What should be the behavior and character of a Christian who can serve as a microcosm of a congregation which is itself a microcosm of the macro-macrocosm of the kingdom of God? The question, of course, takes in much more territory than we can hope to cover here. The whole New Testament (the whole Bible for that matter) is, in one sense, an answer. The answer, of course, must include all aspects of both faith and discipleship, and many books have been written on each of these aspects. But rather than trying to duplicate them, our effort will be to identify the general, overall characteristic that is the trademark of all these detailed actions. Then we will talk a little about how we might go about incorporating this trademark into our lives.

The best name for this trademark is "Christian simplicity." I insist upon including the adjective "Christian" as well as the noun "simplicity," because there are some understandings of and approaches to simplicity that do not qualify at all. However, even before we come to individual lifestyle, it may be that "Christian simplicity" is the best description for the distinction between the two types of congregations. A caravan is certainly more simply organized than a commissary. *Expediti* represent a simpler line of authority and control than does an avant-garde. Barbershopping is a simpler way of making music than staging the Royal Vienna String Quartet. To live unmindful of class is more simple than to be continually striving for it. Making church decisions through communal counsel is more simple than making decisions through management charts. And fidelity (finding a single focus and becoming wholly obedient to it) is more simple, although not easier, than success (which inevitably involves playing all the angles). Indeed, it is fidelity itself which makes Christian simplicity distinctively Christian.

It may be, of course, that some of these congregational simplicities are directly applicable to microcosmic behavior as well. Nevertheless, we want here to stress that simplicity of individual lifestyle affects conduct in every area, at points that might not even occur to us on first thought. Indeed, I am reluctant to list examples, lest they be taken as exhaustive, and implications for other aspects of life be ignored.

Undoubtedly the sort of items that first come to mind at the mention of simplicity have to do with our possessions and material goods — fashionable clothing, gourmet food, luxurious dwellings, expensive recreations and vacations, fine vehicles, appliances and conveniences, and cosmetics and adornments (you extend the list). However, we need also to consider simplicity in some other, very different situations. How about simplifying the pace and multiplicity of our involvements in activities, our "go-go-go" mentality? How about simplifying our personal relationships, clearing out all the superfluities of title, rank, status, and prestige, and just being people for a change? How about listening to Jesus when he says, "Let what you say be simply 'Yes' or 'No'; anything more than this comes from evil" (Mt. 5:37), and do away, not only with oaths, but also with flattery, overblown rhetoric, and salesmanship "come-ons"? How about simplifying our faith by neither spinning it out into highly-intellectualized theories, nor into complicated charts revealing the future of the universe?

What is our next step? Perhaps some may want to know *how* to go about making these simplifications in order to be better microcosms, but that is the wrong request. It overlooks the most crucial aspect of the whole procedure. You see, fidelity to Jesus is not always the motive behind "simplification." A person can be motivated by his or her desire for success — which is something quite different from fidelity. Thus a person could become more simple in every area we have talked about and still not be any closer to *Christian* simplicity. Fidelity means doing something because we are following Jesus, because he *asks* us to. Success means doing something in order to achieve some goal or realize some value without regard to Jesus' will or command.

In the case of simple living, the foremost argument is that simplicity constitutes the most *satisfying* life, simplicity can successfully bring happiness. That may be true (although I am sure that for many people it would not be), and I am not saying that there is anything wrong in seeking happiness.

Let us simplify our lives, then, in order to save food, goods, and money that can be given to the poor. The gospel does obligate us to have a concern about poverty and world hunger. Nevertheless, many non-Christian humanitarians (and even governmental agencies) share that concern; thus helping the poor does not prove that one is acting out of Christian discipleship. Jacques Ellul has made a rather startling comment in this regard. He contends that a broad, generalized benevolence toward faraway people en masse (e.g., "the starving children of the world") — even if it means contributing money, giving up a few meals, or walking for the hungry — cannot be called Christian love, or *agapé*. No, that must involve truly *personal* knowledge, mutuality, and response. Certainly, Ellul would contend that the practice of this broad benevolence is a good thing, but he would deny that doing it makes one a Christian.

Then perhaps we ought to simplify our lives for *ecological* reasons, so that we might succeed in passing on to our children and grandchildren an environment that is liveable and has sufficient resources. This is, in every way, a good idea, and one for which we could find scriptural backing. Yet the ecological arguments are just as applicable to non-Christians. Many people who *are* simplifying their lives out of ecological considerations (and many of the organizations supporting them) make no Christian profession at all. Christians *should* practice good ecology but that in itself does not make them Christians.

We have not named all the possible motives for simplifying our lives. Some of them are probably good and true. Even so, none represents the "what do ye more than others?" Where, then, does the answer lie? With Jesus, obviously — and that most particularly in the Sermon on the Mount, where he focuses on the simple life.

According to him, there is only one basic simplicity, one *extraordinary* simplicity. All our other simplicities are to depend upon it; it is to be the source of all other simplicities. Jesus, we will see, speaks to this point time after time, in many different ways, but his most succinct and pointed statement (a verse we have already used in another context) comes as the summary of the simple-life passage, Matthew 6:19-34.

> *Set your mind on God's kingdom and his justice before everything else, and all the rest will come to you as well.* —Matthew 6:33

This is the authoritative definition of fidelity and simplicity. There is a "first," and there is an "all the rest." The gospel never attempts to deny the reality or validity of the "all the rest," for in this comes the possibility of the successes and accomplishments of a more satisfying life in helping the poor, becoming ecologically responsible, and so forth. Nevertheless, a hard and fast distinction ought to be maintained between the "first" and "all the rest"; no confusion can be allowed.

The all-controlling consideration must be that the "first" actually is made first and maintained as first. Once that is done, "all the rest" can follow behind, find its place, and assume true value and authenticity. This is Christianity's "simple life."

And in this instance, the old saying of "putting first things first" is not quite good enough. The New Testament makes it evident that "first" is singular and not plural; "putting *the first thing* first" would be the only proper way to state this. Kierkegaard has a book entitled *Purity of Heart Is to Will One Thing.* It could as well have been called (and Kierkegaard would not object) *The Simple Life Is to Will One Thing.* But in that book he makes the point that only the "first" that Jesus specifies can be put first and remain only *one* thing. Anything else that might be taken out of the "all the rest" and set up as "first" will inevitably result in double-mindedness rather than a single focus. And here is the ultimate simplicity from which all other simplicities must spring, namely, a *single* focus of life, a single authority, a single center, a single lordship.

"Set your mind on God's kingdom and his justice before everything else," Jesus tells us. That might seem to be a double focus; in actuality, it is not. "God's kingdom" does not designate a location or any outward object. His *kingdom* is his "kingness," the *de facto* situation of his being *king,* the exercising of his proper rule. Thus, "to set one's mind upon his kingdom" is to seek, above all, to let the king's will be done in one's life, to put oneself into appropriate relationship to him as a subject.

That we are to seek God's "justice" (righteousness), on the other hand, does not, in the first place (and we are concerned here particularly with "the first place," you will recall), invite us to try to bring the affairs of men into that arrangement we feel God would deem "just"; this, properly, is part of the "all the rest that will come to you as well." No, in the first place, God's "justice" is *his own* activity of getting things straightened out and made right, his own "just-making action." Thus, "to set one's mind upon his justice" is to relate to him in such a way that he can make *you* right — "let him have his way with thee," as the old hymn has it. This means, of course, that one must approach him as true and sovereign Lord; and God's kingdom and his justice turn out to be two words pointing to one reality, one relationship. The one thing that must be "first" is *fidelity*, that is, absolute, personal loyalty.

But we must be careful to understand what it means to be faithful, to obey one's Lord. If I do everything he has in mind, but do it because I happen to agree that what he has suggested is the intelligent and appropriate thing to do, then I am not obeying *him*. I am merely obeying my own good sense and judgment. In such a case, the *principle* under which I am operating would say that I am to obey only as long as his commands strike me as being right and proper. And this is not putting God's kingdom and justice before everything else; it is putting *myself* first — my judgments, my ideas of good and bad and right and wrong.

"Doing the will of God," then, does not mean simply doing what he wants done; it means doing it "because" *he* wants it done. And that is entirely a matter of *inner* motivation. Only the life that springs from this inner motivation of personal fidelity to the Lord God is true *Christian* simplicity.

Time after time in his Sermon on the Mount, Jesus stresses the importance of inner motivation:

> *Do not store up for yourselves treasure on earth, where it grows rusty and moth-eaten, and thieves break in to steal it. Store up treasure in heaven, where there is no moth and no rust to spoil it, no thieves to break in and steal. For where your treasure is, there will your heart be also.* —Matthew 6:19-21

Your "treasure" is that to which you ascribe preeminent value. And what could "treasure in heaven" be except valuing God himself and one's personal relationship to him? This treasure, by the way, can be enjoyed even before one is "in heaven." And, we are told, it is upon *this* treasure that we are to put our hearts.

> *The lamp of the body is the eye. If your eyes are sound [single], you will have light for your whole body; if the eyes are bad, your whole body will be in darkness. If then the only light you have is darkness, the darkness is doubly dark.*
> —Matthew 6:22-23

A person's vision, the illumination of his entire existence, depends entirely upon the focus of his eye (his fidelity commitment). If that focus is not sound and single, not totally upon God, then everything else in this world will accordingly be darkened. The eye ("I") must be right if anything is rightly to be seen.

> *No servant can be the slave of two masters; for either he will hate the first and love the second or he will be devoted to the first and*

> *think nothing of the second. You cannot serve God and
> Money.* —*Matthew 6:24*

Instead of "God and Money," we have been saying "Fidelity
and Success," but the thought is the same. One's ultimate loyalty
must converge at a single point. To try to go two ways at once will
divide a person down the middle and make his life multi-manic
rather than simple.

> *THEREFORE I bid you put away anxious thoughts about food
> and drink to keep you alive, and clothes to cover your body. . . .
> All these are things for the heathen to run after, not for you,
> because your heavenly Father knows that you need them all. Set
> your mind on God's kingdom and his justice before everything
> else, and all the rest will come to you as well.*
> —*Matthew 6:25, 32-33*

The twelfth chapter of Matthew marks a second concentra-
tion on the theme and includes further implications.

> *Every kingdom divided against itself goes to ruin; and no town, no
> household, that is divided against itself can stand.*
> —*Matthew 12:25*

> *He who is not with me is against me, and he who does not gather
> with me scatters.* —*Matthew 12:30*

We should note a difference between this last saying and
those that have preceded it. For the most part Jesus speaks of our
loyalty being directed *to God*, although at times, as here, he speaks
of loyalty *toward himself*. The remainder of the New Testament (as
our own study here) tends to speak of loyal discipleship *to Jesus*.

Actually, there is no conflict at all here because, throughout
the New Testament, Jesus is presented as being the Christ, the
anointed one, the one whom God has *chosen* as the agent of his
own presence among men. Thus, when someone wants to be loyal
to God, God, as it were, points to Jesus and says, "Very good; and
my desire is that you express your loyalty to me by becoming a true
disciple of his." And if someone chooses to make Jesus his Lord and
dedicate himself loyally to him, Jesus says, "Fine; but to be loyal to
me you must be entirely loyal to God as I myself am." There is no
way the two loyalties can get out of balance, because they are, in
fact, one loyalty.

Later in the chapter from Matthew, Jesus restates his theme:

"Who is my mother? Who are my brothers?"; and pointing to the disciples, he said, "Here are my mother and my brothers. Whoever does the will of my heavenly Father is my brother, my sister, my mother."—Matthew 12:48-50

For Jesus, this fidelity in doing the will of God so entirely takes precedence over everything else that the person who practices it comes closer to and rates higher with him than do his own mother, brothers, and sisters.

In the succeeding chapter of Matthew, Jesus stresses the great importance of undivided commitment by presenting twin parables regarding the kingdom of heaven. Recall that this "kingdom of heaven" is God himself affirmed in his kingly ruling.

The kingdom of heaven is like treasure lying buried in a field. The man who found it, buried it again; and for sheer joy went and sold everything he had, and bought that field.

Here is another picture of the kingdom of heaven. A merchant looking for fine pearls found one of very special value; so he went and sold everything he had, and bought it. —Matthew 13:44-46

In Luke's Gospel, Jesus pointedly states:

No one who sets his hand to the plough and then keeps looking back is fit for the kingdom of God. —Luke 9:62

Any simplicity that looks elsewhere than solely to kingdom fidelity is not the kind of plowing advocated by the gospel.

Christian simplicity, then (for we are finally to the place that a definition is in order), is that style of life which grows out of and bears the fruit of a commitment of total fidelity to Jesus Christ. It is the effort to find the character and behavior that will best give expression to the fact that such fidelity means more to me than success, accomplishment, satisfaction, or whatever else might make up the "all the rest."

And this Christian simplicity, it is most important to say, involves more than just my personal effort to get my own priorities right; it is a means of public witness — of evangelism — if you will. It is a means by which others can be shown that the gospel (and my life in the gospel) is centered in the lordship of Jesus rather than in fine buildings (even if dedicated to Christ), possessions, worldly satisfactions, and so forth. Any lifestyle that gives people the impression that I value anything else as much or more than I value being obedient to Jesus Christ proclaims a false gospel.

Now I know that many readers would like me to get specific about a life of Christian simplicity. "What can a Christian own, and what can he not own? How much can he pay for a house without compromising simplicity?" No one can answer those questions, because Christian simplicity has to be the fruit of individual fidelity to Jesus. Such fidelity is an intensely personal matter, and the results will reflect the individuality of each person and situation. Of course, some *general* observations and counsels could be made. But we have in mind to do something better. In the next chapter we will discuss how best to go about getting answers to the question "What shall I do?"

But there is a final consideration needed in this chapter. "Although it would seem good that the right things are done for the right reasons, what real difference does it make as long as the right thing is done in the end? Getting our lives simplified is what we are after here, so if one person does it out of fidelity to Jesus and another does it out of other motives, what does it matter? You get simplicity either way, don't you?"

Well, that sounds logical (and it may be), but it is not true! For one thing, the simplicity dedicated to Jesus should and will be publicly *attributed* to him, thus becoming a witness that otherwise-motivated simplicity can never be. Yet the distinction goes much deeper than that.

"Motives" cannot be counted as one thing and the "outcome" as something entirely different. The motive of any action carries over and is incorporated into the outcome whether its presence is readily apparent or not. Thus, identical actions, which seem as though they should produce identical outcomes, may have entirely different meanings and results if done out of different motives.

For instance, any venture with the goal of success necessarily involves an action that can be counted upon to produce the desired outcome. The most that is wanted from the action, then, is that it bring about the desired result. The venture neither envisions nor desires the involvement of factors other than those of cause-and-effect calculation.

The case is quite different with ventures aimed at fidelity. There is now no calculation designed for a pre-selected outcome. The only interest is in being obedient. However, to be obedient to Jesus is to invite *him* into the action. The outcome now is in his hands, and that makes it entirely incalculable. That outcome may turn out to be what would have happened anyway, yet there is always the possibility that the Lord may choose to do something quite different with it, something quite different from what we would have chosen as success, yet also something much greater than mere success — namely, a bit of the coming of the kingdom. No one can say what fidelity will bring; but it certainly is not limited to mere success.

So give Christian simplicity a try. Become a simple microcosm, and see what happens!

SEVEN

Stripping and Other Meaningful Activities You Can Do in Church

We started this book by examining the style of the Christian *congregation*. In the preceding chapter we moved to the style of the Christian *individual*. But now we want to combine our two foci and examine what the Christian individual can and should be doing *within* the congregation. How does the microcosm function within the macrocosm? How do the members operate together as the body of Christ?

Again, our discussion admittedly must be very limited. Surely it must be obvious that a member's method of operation will be quite different according to whether his church is a caravan or a commissary. Yet, of course, each type has the same kinds of activities: worship, the sacraments, Christian education, Bible study, business meetings, fellowship, evangelism, and service outreach. Our earlier discussion has shown how the individual's involvement in these will differ depending upon congregational orientation. (And it might be a good exercise to go through the list and define the differences.) Even so, almost all congregations are aware of and working at these activities.

Our focus now will be on neglected activities which hardly are possibilities for the commissary congregation but which can and should be of central importance in the caravan congregation.

The first example is directly related to simplicity that was the theme of our previous chapter. We insisted that simplicity will need to grow out of the particular situation of each individual (or family). We still stand by that but now add that individualized simplicity can best be accomplished (perhaps *only* be ac-

83

complished) with the counsel and help of "the brethren"— one's
brothers and sisters in the community. We need this sharing,
whether it can be done with the congregation as a whole or must
take place in smaller groups.

In the first place, through worship, Bible study, and discussion, we need to help each other remember our *motives* for simplifying our life style. It is so easy to forget and to slip into the purely
secular interests of saving money and seeking happiness.

In the second place, a number of people working together,
pooling their expertise, experience, and time, can do a much
better job in sifting through the countless simplification suggestions and ideas available from secular sources. The group can
share, evaluate, and test these suggestions, and help one another
to seek first the kingdom of God when implementing them. In a
word, we need the help of one another in preserving the "more
than" of our endeavor.

Finally, there is a great deal of simplification we can achieve
by actually working together. We can discover mutual helpfulness
(and helpfulness to those who are not in a position to reciprocate).
We can exchange expert advice and services (from babysitting to
auto repair). We can pool the use of equipment rather than each
family having to acquire its own equipment. We might even join
together to do quantity buying. Cooperation as a form of simplification has the added advantage of promoting true community. But
yet once more we must caution that seeking first the simple life is
not the equivalent of seeking first the kingdom of God.

A second neglected but necessary activity of members
within the body is mutual discipline. There is no denying that
discipline is a central element in the New Testament view of the
faith community. The golden text is Hebrews 12:5-11:

> You have forgotten the text of Scripture which addresses you as
> sons and appeals to you in these words:
> "My son, do not think lightly of the Lord's discipline,
> nor lose heart when he corrects you;
> for the Lord disciplines those whom he loves;
> he lays the rod on every son whom he acknowledges."
> You must endure it as discipline: God is treating you as sons. Can
> anyone be a son, who is not disciplined by his father? If you escape
> the discipline in which all sons share, you must be bastards and not

true sons. Again, we paid due respect to the earthly fathers who disciplined us; should we not submit even more readily to our spiritual Father, and so attain life? They disciplined us for this short life according to their lights; but he does so for our true welfare, so that we may share his holiness. Discipline, no doubt, is never pleasant; at the time it seems painful, but in the end it yields for those who have been trained by it the peaceful harvest of an honest life.

Goodness knows there is little discipline in our churches. In a commissary church, discipline normally comes from the top down, as the commissars, acting by the book (the denomination's canons of polity), work to keep the "non-coms" and troops in line.

But discipline is even more crucial in a caravan, where each caravaner has to play his proper part if the venture is to go at all. Caravan discipline also comes from the top, but in an entirely different sense. Notice that the Hebrews text speaks entirely and exclusively of *the Lord's* disciplining *a son.* And because a caravan consists solely of "brethren" (brothers and sisters undistinguished as to rank), there is no one in it who has the right or authority to discipline another.

In 2 Corinthians 2:1-11 and 7:8-13, Paul relates an incident that reveals his understanding of church discipline. A situation had arisen in the Corinthian congregation that called for Paul's on-the-spot presence. The trouble apparently centered on one person (2:5-8; 7:12: "the one who did wrong"). Whatever his original misdeed, it obviously came to include face-to-face defiance of Paul and a rejection of his apostolic status. Paul entered the situation as an apostle and with a keen apprehension of what that implied — in the church of that day there was no higher human authority than an apostle.

Yet evidence shows that neither Paul nor the congregation understood that awesome "authority" as including official or ecclesiastical clout. Paul was unable (or did not see it as his prerogative) either to silence or to oust the offender from fellowship. Paul was hurt by the congregation's failure to support him, "pained by those who should have made me rejoice, for I felt sure of all of you" (2:3). But he never accuses them of refusing to enforce an apostolic decree. The confrontation was what Paul calls a "painful visit" (2:1) and entirely fruitless.

After he left Corinth, Paul wrote a letter (2:3, 4, 9; 7:8, 12) to the Corinthians (which was not preserved). After reading Paul's letter, the Corinthians outdid themselves in expressing their love and support for Paul and in proving "themselves guiltless in the matter" (7:11). The congregation itself acted to punish the recalcitrant individual (presumably by ousting him from fellowship — 2:6), and apparently that action had succeeded in winning his repentance: "So you should rather turn to forgive and comfort him, or he may be overwhelmed by excessive sorrow. So I beg you to reaffirm your love for him. . . . Any one whom you forgive, I also forgive" (2:7-10).

This is a beautiful story. But its prickly point is that, although this church had offices (from apostles on down), these did not constitute the pyramidal hierarchy of authority or the enforceable chain of command that the commissary church, so soon after, made central to its structural efficiency. The most apostolically-minded apostle of them all deliberately declined to exercise the authority of his position either in punishing the troublemaker or in declaring him forgiven (Paul simply adds his forgiveness to that of the rest of the congregation).

It would seem, then, that Paul advocates complete parity between members of a body: "But God has so adjusted the body, giving the greater honor to the inferior part, that there may be no discord in the body, but that the members may have the same care for one another" (1 Cor. 12:24-25). Not only do Christians have a parity of status in the eyes of God (as generally understood in Paul's text), but they also have parity under God's discipline. The ultimate source of command, certainly, is the head, Christ Jesus himself. But he has not deputized this authority to other individuals. Any "commanding" that needs to be done is an action of the body.

And the same understanding would seem to be reflected in Matthew 18:15-17, our most explicit counsel on the procedures of church discipline:

> If your brother sins against you, go and tell him his fault, between you and him alone. If he listens to you, you have gained your brother. But if he does not listen, take one or two others along with you, that every word may be confirmed by the evidence of two or three witnesses. If he refuses to listen to them, tell it to the church;

*and if he refuses to listen even to the church, let him be to you as a
Gentile and a tax collector.*

There is no hint here of the existence of officers or hierarchical
authorities who ought to intervene to discipline people. (And
although these are reported as the words of *Jesus*, Matthew is
addressing them as counsel to churches of the eighties, after the
time of Paul. The church without rank cannot be dismissed as a
very early and short-lived phase.)

If Paul had been willing to organize Corinth the way we
organize churches today, the proper officials (even Paul himself)
early would have stepped in to nip the trouble in the bud and thus
prevent all the agony. Whether they would also have been able to
redeem the erring brother is a moot question. But Paul would rather
endure Corinth and all the internal tempestuousness of his
churches, and thus preserve Christian freedom and parity, than to
sacrifice those in exchange for the managerial efficiency of our
commissaries. And Paul is right.

The brethren are not to discipline the individual; that is
God's responsibility. However, they can and should be supporters,
helpers, and enablers in the process going on between the individual and his Lord. And that process, by the way, does not
begin when an individual gets out of line. No, *true* discipline (like
the father's discipline of a son) is preventive discipline, that is,
helping the individual keep in line so that he does not get out of
line.

Consequently, each Christian is being disciplined by God all
the time. The congregation is not divided into those who are being
disciplined and those who are helping discipline others. No,
everyone is to be doing both, or to be continually alternating from
one role to the other. Selecting out a person for special discipline is
only an emergency measure, and the better job we do at continual,
preventive disciplining, the fewer occasions we will have for
emergency measures.

Christian discipline is meant to be self-discipline, although
that is actually a contradiction in terms. *Self-discipline* cannot mean
doing what the self directs at the moment; that would not be
discipline at all. What the term intends, then, is *voluntary* discipline as over against *imposed* discipline. And this certainly fits

Christianity, for the Lord does not impose himself on anyone. Jesus becomes my Lord when I accept him as Lord. He calls, but I am not a disciple until I have made a free commitment to follow (which commitment, by the way, also includes promises and obligations regarding the community, the body of Christ). The congregation, then, is constituted solely of those who are committed to this self-discipline — the free decision of having taken Jesus as Lord.

Notice, also, that the Hebrews text emphasizes that God's discipline is a discipline of *love* (as toward a *son*, not an *enemy*) and that it is always for "our true welfare," "the peaceful harvest of an honest life."

It would seem, then, that we can be most helpful in the matter of God's discipline by keeping each other reminded that we are under this discipline, that we have said that we wanted Jesus as Lord, that we have volunteered for the shaping, molding, and sandpapering that will make us what God wants us to be. By pointing out to my brother those areas in his life which appear to be resistant or closed to God's approach, I may help him to become more open to God. And of course, the best way to encourage him is to show that I am also ready to welcome his observations about me. Above all, our mutual efforts must always communicate the qualities of God's discipline and love.

And let us never overlook what is without doubt the very best means of cooperating under God's discipline: Bible study — though of a very special sort. It probably needs to happen in smaller, more intimate groups than those of customary classes. In addition the attention should not be exclusively on *the text:* "How did it come to be? What form does it represent? What does each of the words mean? What theological perspective does it reflect?" Rather, the focus must be on ourselves: "What is God saying *to me* through these words? How do these words judge me? What do they ask of me? What changes would God have them work in me?" In this way, the word itself, communicated through the insights, mutuality, and love of the brethren, can begin to make God's discipline personal, real, and effective.

I do not deny that there can and do arise nasty Corinthian-type situations that call for more stringent (though no less loving) discipline. When one caravaner (or group of caravaners) pulls off in such a divergent direction so as to jeopardize the caravan itself, when he refuses to admit that his direction is divergent, and when he refuses to hear either the brethren or the word that God would speak through them — when this happens, Scripture indicates that God's discipline can be drastic, and it directs the congregation to support God's hand in this as in the other. But the tragedy of the church is that, out of distaste for facing up to nasty situations, we have identified discipline entirely with these emergency measures and therefore abjured *all* discipline — the normal as well as the drastic. The result is that we live (in the words of the author of Hebrews) more like bastards than as God's true sons.

Now we turn to the activity you have probably been wondering about since you noticed the title of this chapter — stripping. This activity is closely related to discipline in that stripping may be a pre-condition of discipline, or at least a vital aspect of it.

Let us begin by defining stripping. We have in mind the action of a person baring himself psychologically, emotionally, spiritually — divesting himself of his facade, role-playing, false modesty (and false pride) — anything that veils self-honesty. Indeed, much of modern psychology and counseling (in and out of the church) promotes such stripping as "salvation," or at least the way to salvation.

I disagree with this view. If one strips before a professional psyche-observer or a group of peering peers, there may be a certain temporary cathartic effect for the stripper, but nothing worth the risks involved. This kind of stripping is no different from strip-teasing. The stripper is an "exhibitionist," concerned only with showing off and seducing others rather than learning any truth about himself. Likewise, the observers are "voyeurs" interested more in the gratification of seeing the other's secrets than in being of any help to him. This sort of relationship, of course, does no one any good. However, under the guise of "sensitivity training," "consciousness raising," or "small-group sharing," a good deal of it has gone on and is going on in our churches.

The only stripping that avoids perversion and opens positive alternatives is that done *before God*. Psalm 139 (among many similar ones) is the best expression of what we have in mind:

Yahweh, you examine me and know me,
you know if I am standing or sitting,

you read my thoughts from far away,
whether I walk or lie down, you are watching,
you know every detail of my conduct.

It was you who created my inmost self,
and put me together in my mother's womb;
for all these mysteries I thank you:
for the wonder of myself, for the wonder of your works.

God, how hard it is to grasp your thoughts!
How impossible to count them!
I could no more count them than I could the sand,
and suppose I could, you would still be with me.

God, examine me and know my heart,
probe me and know my thoughts;
make sure I do not follow pernicious ways,
and guide me in the way that is everlasting.
                    —Psalm 139:1-3, 13:14, 17-18, 23-24
                    (Jerusalem Bible)

This, I suppose, is what has been customarily called confession rather than stripping. I have changed the term to get away from the idea of simply listing the bad things one has said, thought, and done, and having a professional religionist assure one of forgiveness or a professional psychologist assure one that these things weren't bad to begin with. In the opening-out I am speaking of, there may be revealed some things which are much worse than everyday sins and some things which are grounds for thanksgiving, wonder, and praise.

Kierkegaard pointed out that our purpose in revealing ourselves to God is not that he might learn something about us, but that from him we might learn something we have not known, or have not been willing to face, about ourselves. The Psalmist agrees completely. Once we have found out, with God's help we are also ready to be helped out. Because he is present and active, God can make sure that I do not follow pernicious ways, but instead follow the way that is everlasting.

Obviously, stripping is an intensely personal action of the individual before God and not before the brethren. Yet, I did not say private. In this instance, as in our earlier ones, personal experience can best take place (perhaps even *must* take place) within the context of community. Thus, in this case, although I do not strip *before* the brethren, I ought to strip *with* my brethren *before* God. The Psalmist himself points us in this direction by doing his own stripping in the form of a public, written account, undoubtedly intended as encouragement to his brethren.

The first way the community can help is by reminding me that I need the stripping experience. Furthermore, the greatest encouragement for me to do it is to discover that my brothers and sisters are willing to bare themselves with me. Also, that we can do this with one another in love keeps me aware that God's attitude toward me is one of love.

Beyond this mutual helpfulness there is an even more basic consideration. As long as my stripping is done in complete privacy before God, there is always the suspicion (it should be my own suspicion) that I have not truly nor completely stripped at all. It is too easy to say that I have opened every aspect of my life to God when that is not really the case. To verbalize these things in the presence of other people helps keep me honest and also gives God an opportunity to verbalize, *through them,* his love and forgiveness *toward me.*

This mutuality of stripping before God may be the most important activity of the Christian community, related as it is to the forgiveness of sin; yet it is also the most precarious and difficult activity. It can so easily become exhibitionism or voyeurism; and our only protection is that we focus it wholly upon God and do it only under his direction.

The three congregational activities we have examined — mutual aid in simplifying our lifestyles, mutual helpfulness in applying God's discipline, and the mutual baring of our selves to God — are not actually distinct and separate works. They may even be ascending steps, each making the next possible. In any case, they amount to a basic aspect of discipleship, and they are a basic part of the church's calling. They also point to a basic lack in the life of the modern church and the experience of modern Christians.

None of these three activities can be accomplished in the way the church normally accomplishes activities. They do not happen through committee decision, organizational goal-setting, staff programming, or the budgeting of funds (although actions at this level can either encourage or thwart the process). All three activities (in ascending degree) must occur in a group with a strong sense of community (*koinonia*), an intimate "feel" for one another, a deep sense of trust in one another, and a firm commitment to caravan with one another. Most congregations do not have the base from which to pursue these activities, even if they wanted to. Although this sense of community is both the motive and the product of the caravan church, it is in no sense a human, sociological creation. It is a gift of God and, more than that, a grace that comes only through being in Jesus Christ and truly letting that action incorporate us as his body.

EIGHT

A Meditation on Ellul's Inutility

As an appendix or afterthought to his book *The Politics of God and the Politics of Man,* Jacques Ellul wrote a piece entitled "Meditation on Inutility." It is one of the most unsettling and devastating passages of Christian writing ever done, yet it is very difficult (I would say impossible) to argue with it biblically.

My opinion is that the meditation would be more appropriate as a conclusion to this book than to Ellul's; at least it will have a somewhat broader application here. So what I propose is a meditation on Ellul's "Meditation on Inutility," which will not only summarize what he had to say, but will also adapt his thoughts to fit this particular study.

In *Politics* (though perhaps more so in some of his other books), Ellul observes how preoccupied modern society is with activism and accomplishment. The only purpose of both social and personal life is to get things done. Success (as we have used the term in this book and as it is used generally) has but one meaning: to set goals and accomplish them — or at least be on the way to accomplishing them. The worth of a society and every group or organization within it is measured by what it has done and what difference it has made in the world. One's self-worth is found only in what one has done with his or her life, and what one has to show for it.

Also in *Politics,* Ellul observes that in this regard, modern Christians are no different from anyone else. We, of course, are called to accomplish things for God, but the dictum that you are not much of anything unless you are *doing* something holds true

93

even in Christian circles. The hymn "Rise Up, O Men of God" may be in disrepute because of its alleged sexism, but it is still the quintessence of what the modern church preaches, teaches, writes, demonstrates, belabors, and hints: "Come on, let's get up and be about all these things God wants accomplished!"

In his "Meditation on Inutility," Ellul submits this axiom — so taken for granted that we never thought to question it — to the test of Scripture. The results are very interesting.

In Genesis 2:8 we are told:

> Then the Lord God planted a garden in Eden away to the east, and there he put the man whom he had formed. The Lord God made trees spring from the ground, all trees pleasant to look at and good for food; and in the middle of the garden he set the tree of life and the tree of knowledge of good and evil.

And yet, just a few verses later, God commands Adam to *till the ground and care for it.* What on earth for? We had just been told that things were growing like nobody's business (God's business, but nobody else's). Tilling the ground and caring for it appears to be a completely useless task, yet God asks Adam to do it.

Ellul, then, quickly brings the matter more closely home. Both the Old Testament and the New are full of laws or commands of God regarding the observance of rites, our behavior, and what we are to do and not do. The gospel then proclaims that we are saved entirely by grace and not by the merit of any sort of works. What, then, is the point of hard-earned righteousness? What did it accomplish? These are all seemingly useless tasks, yet God commands us to do them.

What about prayer? God knows what we need before we ask. When we do pray, according to Romans 8:26, it is the Holy Spirit who does the praying for us. God can do everything that needs to be done or he wants done, whether we pray or not. This seems like an entirely useless business, yet God asks us to pray.

What about wisdom — man's intelligent efforts at planning, ordering, and rationalizing life? The book of Proverbs is one grand call for men to find and to practice wisdom. Yet, in 1 Corinthians 1:20-27, Paul says:

> Where are any of our thinkers today? Do you see how God has shown up the foolishness of human wisdom? If it was God's

wisdom that human wisdom should not know God, it was because God wanted to save those who have faith through the foolishness of the message that we preach. . . . For God's foolishness is wiser than human wisdom, and God's weakness is stronger than human strength. Take yourselves for instance, brothers, at the time when you were called: how many of you were wise in the ordinary sense of the word, how many were influential people, or came from noble families?

Here we are not invited to quit trying for wisdom — any more than we are invited to quit praying, obeying, or tilling. We are to do these things, yes, but we must not think that it accomplishes anything more than God could accomplish by himself.

Finally, Ellul speaks of preaching. Paul considered preaching a great obligation: "Woe to me if I do not preach the gospel" (1 Cor. 9:16). And yet he knew as well as anyone that no human words have the power to convict men of sin and change their lives. It is the Holy Spirit who does those things, and the Spirit does not depend on any particular individual or his sermons. If the person is silent, the Spirit can get the word out through someone else or in some other way. So one can preach, yes, but it also is essentially useless.

Let me now go beyond Ellul and become more personal — as an encouragement for you to make the line of thought more personal. I have now taught religion in college for more than twenty years. I have been teaching the word without end (my teaching has been without end; the students themselves find an end easily enough, namely, as soon as they can get out the door or at least receive a grade). I have pounded pulpits and podiums, not only in my own congregation, but all over the country, preaching until I was blue in the face and audiences seemingly were completely unconscious. I have published approximately one book a year for the past decade. Publishers have invested thousands of dollars in making these writings available. An infinitely greater accomplishment is that people like yourselves have spent even more money buying them.

Now, can all that be called "useless"? Surely it ought to count for something? And it does: I can show you entries in different *Who's Whos* to prove it. But that is only one way of looking at my career. The other way is more honest.

Can I claim that the world is more Christian because of my contribution? Is the world a perceptibly better place because of me? Is the kingdom of God more fully present or nearer at hand because of what I have done? At this very moment I am writing a book that challenges the whole modern church and calls for a radically different sort of congregational structure and life — do I really think this book will make any discernible difference in the character of American Christendom? Or, to put it in a word, what have I ever done for God that he could not have done just as well without me? I do believe that it is God who has given me these tasks, and I intend to continue doing them; but I am under no illusion that God needs me nor that I have made any essential contribution to him. The stirring poem "God Has No Hands But Our Hands" is nothing but froth and fizz.

In saying this, I am not deprecating myself or betraying a low self-image. I would hope that Billy Graham, Martin Luther King, Corrie Ten Boom, or any Christian you could name would be as willing to speak the same way about himself or herself, for I truly believe it is the only honest way. The modern, apparently universal plague of low self-image comes not from this way of thinking. Quite the contrary, a low self-image is a result of the game called "nothing counts but accomplishments," and comes about as people start measuring their accomplishments against those of other people — something that the gospel does not encourage. That Billy Graham's contributions to God are just as useless as mine is precisely the *cure* rather than the *cause* of a low self-image.

Ellul spots the true significance of his thought by going to Luke 17:7-10.

> *Suppose one of you has a servant ploughing or minding sheep. When he comes back from the fields, will the master say, "Come along at once and sit down"? Will he not rather say, "Prepare my supper, fasten your belt, and wait on me while I have my meal; you can have yours afterwards"? Is he grateful to the servant for carrying out his orders? So with you: when you have carried out all your orders, you should say, "We are servants and deserve no credit* [KJV: *"unprofitable servants"*; NAS: *"unworthy slaves"*; CL: *"useless slaves"*]; *we have only done our duty."*

Regarding this text, Ellul makes a couple of crucial observations. First, it is not at the outset, when the orders are given, that the servant has the right to judge the work as being useless and thus can make that an excuse for doing it grudgingly or not at all. It is only "when you have carried out all your orders" that it is proper to say, "I deserve no credit; I have only done my duty." The world has it all wrong in thinking that the desire for accomplishment is the only effective motive for action. A more effective (and much more reliable) motive is to act out of love for God and because he has asked you to undertake a task.

Second, Ellul points out that it is not God or Jesus who pronounces the verdict that we are unprofitable servants. This is an insight that we must realize ourselves. If we were forced to say it, there would be nothing gained, but if we say it voluntarily we will learn a great truth about ourselves and we will grow in discipleship. By doing this, we will discover what Christian discipleship is all about. Jesus does not pronounce your Christian works and disciple-ship useless; you do that. But at that point, the word from Jesus is likely to be, "Well done, good and faithful servant" (Mt. 25:21). When Jesus says this, he is not arguing with you; he is not saying, "Oh, but you did accomplish many worthwhile things!" He is saying, "You were *faithful*, and that is all that is important. If there is to be *success* or *accomplishment*, I will see to it; but that has nothing to do with whether you were faithful or not. Success or failure depends upon many factors, some of them sheer chance, many of them entirely beyond your control. That you were willing to forgo dreams of accomplishment and to obey simply for the sake of obedience was right. Well done, good and *faithful* servant; enter into the joy of your Lord."

Such "useless service," Ellul declares, introduces two ex-traordinary factors into the life of mankind, factors that are indeed essential to the salvation of the world. First, that my service is "useless" demonstrates that the accomplishment that does come is a gift of *grace* rather than a product of wise human calculation and action. How better can one witness to grace than to say, "It wasn't *my* doing; he did it without me and even in spite of me"?

Further, Ellul declares, a "useless" act is a *free* act, an act which introduces freedom into a world that knows nothing of it otherwise. If the world demands success (and that anything which is not success is failure), then it also is demanding that I do whatever is necessary to produce success. And where is the freedom (where even any *room* for freedom) in that? But because Christian "uselessness" was never dedicated to success, it cannot be failure (you can't miss a mark you weren't shooting at). It is a *free* act done for no other reason than the desire to do it. Of course, the reason I wanted to do that particular act was because it was what God wanted me to do. But I choose to do it in freedom. I chose what God wanted me to do because I *wanted* to do it. He did not force me into that commitment. According to an ancient prayer, God is the one "whose service is perfect freedom."

The supreme example of Ellul's "inutility" is the cross. That cross *had* to be an act of the faithful servant, because it definitely was not a calculation aimed at *accomplishment.* What, in actuality, did the cross accomplish?

(1) It accomplished the death of Jesus — and he would have remained dead had it not been for the resurrection, itself a new act of God and not in any sense a *product* of the crucifixion. (2) It put an end to any thought that Jesus was the Messiah. Without the resurrection there would never have been any more speculation on that score. (3) It marked the end of Jesus' cause and following (the disciples scattered, as they thought, for good), and shortly would have marked the end of all memory of him. (4) It represented the victory of *evil* over good, *hate* over love, *politics* over faith. The cross was, indeed, useless action. Yet it was, at the same time, the world's greatest demonstration of *grace* and its truest witness to *freedom* ("I lay down my life that I may take it again. No one takes it from me, but I lay it down of my own accord" [Jn. 10:17-18]).

And when, as a disciple, I am called to take up my cross and follow him, should I consider *my* action any *more* useful than *his*?

In conclusion, then, let us transpose Ellul's meditation into the more particular setting of our study. I can envision Christian individuals (a goodly number of Christian individuals) heeding this word from God and coming to recognize and confess their own inutility. It might not be easy, but ultimately we do know that all flesh is grass, and most of us, if we were honest, would have to recognize that we have not done much that could count as accomplishment before God. Yes, Jesus' point about our not deserving credit and having only done our duty is correct.

However, I can hardly imagine that any congregations will ever make that admission. "Churches just don't grow *that* way!" —

which is probably true. But the congregation is an organization, and the only reason for organization is to get things done. "And you would ask us to stand up before the world and confess that all our investment and activity has been *useless?* Why, that would be the end of the church!" Wrong! That would be the beginning of the church.

Apparently, this is not what the church (any church) will want to do. No, what we are going to do is build a $27-million crystal cathedral "for the glory of God" (according to the newspaper advertisement). Now I do not know the going rate for God's glory these days, but obviously $27 million worth is nothing to be sneezed at.

"Our campaign resulted in thousands of decisions for Christ. It was probably the greatest event since Pentecost. Don't you try to say that this doesn't count for anything! Of course, we give God the credit for the accomplishment — but it was our techniques, organization, money, and plain hard work that enabled God to do it." Our church has done *this*! Our church has a great program going now in doing *that*! But *our* church is making plans, and we are going to do THAT! And isn't it wonderful, it is all to the glory of God!

What this all comes to is that the modern church simply is not cut out for the unprofitable servant role. But the question remains whether any group not in that role can claim to be the church of Jesus Christ.

What Is It to You?

The postlude is in response to a request from an editor: "We'd like to know exactly what the church should do! Give some specific helps for Christians who want direction in renewing their church." In short, "We've read your book; now tell us what it all means."

I am going to resist the request a bit — as Ellul and Kierkegaard did when the same request was addressed to them — although I do not have the nerve to be as totally obstinate as they were. However, I cannot, and therefore will not, reduce the challenge (which is what I see this book being: a New Testament challenge to the contemporary church) to a checklist of how-to suggestions. Certainly a biblical rebirth of the church will never happen via that route. In the first place, every congregation's circumstances are different enough that no shotgun prescriptions will do. Each church will have to explore its own possibilities and discover God's will in its particular time, place, and situation.

Second, a list of how-to's is not radical enough; it leaves matters on the level of technique-efficiency rather than inviting the Holy Spirit to disrupt lives, thought-patterns, traditions, and structures. (Our age will certainly produce books regarding these topics, e.g., *Techniques for Church Renewal,* or *How to Stage a Pentecost* — as though it lies within *our* powers to manipulate these things into existence!)

I agree with Ellul when he states:

> But I refuse to construct a *system* of thought, or to offer up some Christian or prefabricated socio-political solutions. I want only to provide Christians with the means of thinking

101

out *for themselves* the meaning of their involvement in the modern world.[4]

When, in response to his *Attack Upon 'Christendom'*, Kierkegaard was asked, "What do you want? For what changes are you asking?" his answer was very simple. He denied that he was demanding any changes at all. He was asking for only one thing: honesty. If the church was honest enough to publicly admit that what it was proclaiming (and more importantly, *representing*) as the gospel was not the New Testament gospel of our Lord and Savior Jesus Christ, he would be well satisfied. Now what he knew but did not say was that, if honesty were to force the church into such an embarrassing admission, the embarrassment itself would drive the church back to the New Testament in an effort to get things straightened out.

And I agree with Kierkegaard. If the church simply was honest enough to admit that what it uses as models of a Christian congregation are not the models assigned us in the New Testament, I would be well satisfied — assured, of course, that the admission would initiate healthy changes.

This is probably the most important answer I have to the question asked by the title of this "Postlude." But I do have some additional, more specific, suggestions.

First, to those who are seeking or may in the future be seeking a church home, consider whether Christ may not be calling you into a risk-taking, demanding church membership rather than a safe, spectator one. Why not join a congregation where your presence would make a real difference rather than merely changing a digit or two in already impressive statistics? Why not deliberately put yourself into a situation, the exigencies of which would force you to discover, develop, and exercise gifts you never knew you had and never would have discovered in a larger church? Granted, the prospect of being a member (a foot, a hand, an arm, or a leg) of what is perhaps a "terminally-ill" congregation is not nearly as pleasant or attractive as "taking part" in all the fun and inspiration of an activity-programmed church. But could it not be that Christ calls you to the congregation you can best serve rather than the one that best serves you, to the

[4]In "From Jacques Ellul," a preface to *Introducing Jacques Ellul*, p. 6.

congregation that most needs you rather than the one that best suits your needs? And above all, should not your own fidelity to Christ lead you to look for and value a congregation's fidelity more than its success?

Second, to those who already are in small, struggling, or even terminally-ill congregations, hold up your heads and quit shuffling and snuffling around. Do not allow the classy crowd to force you into buying its models. Quit trying to ape those churches, because you will not be able to pull it off. Look instead to the New Testament and its models, and realize that you actually have all the advantage. It is not that small churches *automatically* fall into the New Testament category, but once they get their priorities straight, they certainly have the easier job of becoming obedient. Success (which they do not have) does not entice them away from their search for fidelity. They can move directly into caravaning, expeditioning, and barbershopping. It will take considerable time and effort for a large congregation to get to that place. The small congregation has much less of a vested interest in the continuance of the world and thus a better chance of getting a focus on the end of the world. Living the risky, tenuous life of a struggling congregation stands one in better stead to hear and understand what the New Testament has to say about the church and to the church. It also helps one to appreciate the truth of Christian inutility. We small-timers have many advantages. Let us thank God for them and use them according to his will.

Finally, to those who are already in large, flourishing churches, I am somewhat baffled as to what to say. I cannot give you any easy formulae, because I do not think there are any. Facing up to the New Testament challenge and becoming honest in relation to it is, of course, the first step for all of us. Beyond that, it certainly is not my place to tell you to move your membership; you will have to deal with your own conscience on that one. Only you can determine how many people in which positions doing what for how long may be required to influence your congregation perceptibly. Obviously, you cannot expect to find any large numbers eager to repudiate their own success and confess congregational inutility. So I guess the word is "chip away" (talk away, study away, pray away); make suggestions and take initiatives when you can. Above all, maintain the vision and be patient in Christian love.

So now to him who by the power at work within us is able to do far more abundantly than all we ask or think, to him be glory in the church and in Christ Jesus to all generations, for ever and ever. Amen.